莎士比亚四大悲剧
英汉对照

Othello

奥 瑟 罗

【英】莎士比亚 著 朱生豪 译

燕山大学出版社
YANSHAN UNIVERSITY PRESS
2018・秦皇岛

图书在版编目（CIP）数据

奥瑟罗：英汉对照 /（英）莎士比亚著；朱生豪译 .—秦皇岛：燕山大学出版社，2018.3（2022.3 重印）

（莎士比亚四大悲剧）

ISBN 978-7-81142-595-6

Ⅰ. ①奥… Ⅱ. ①莎…②朱… Ⅲ. ①英语－汉语－对照读物②悲剧－剧本－英国－中世纪 Ⅳ. ① H319.4：I

中国版本图书馆 CIP 数据核字（2022）第 033045 号

奥瑟罗：英汉对照

（英）莎士比亚著；朱生豪译 .

出 版 人：陈　玉
责任编辑：唐　雷　　　丛书策划：陈　玉　陈亚明
封面设计：金　帆　　　责任印制：吴　波
出版发行：燕山大学出版社 YANSHAN UNIVERSITY PRESS　　　地　址：河北省秦皇岛市河北大街西段 438 号
邮政编码：066004　　　电　话：0335-8387555
印　刷：天津盛奥传媒印务有限公司　　　经　销：全国新华书店

尺　寸：170mm × 240mm　1/16　　印　张：17　　字　数：230 千字
版　次：2018 年 3 月第 1 版　　印　次：2022 年 3 月第 3 次印刷
书　号：ISBN 978-7-81142-595-6
定　价：49.80 元

剧中人物

DUKE OF VENICE 威尼斯公爵

BRABANTIO 勃拉班修：元老

GRATIANO 葛莱西安诺：勃拉班修之弟

LODOVICO 罗多维科：勃拉班修的亲戚

OTHELLO 奥瑟罗：摩尔族贵裔，供职威尼斯政府

CASSIO 凯西奥：奥瑟罗的副将

IAGO 伊阿古：奥瑟罗的旗官

RODERIGO 罗德利哥：威尼斯绅士

MONTANO 蒙太诺：塞浦路斯总督，奥瑟罗的前任者

CLOWN 小丑：奥瑟罗的仆人

DESDEMONA 苔丝狄蒙娜：勃拉班修之女，奥瑟罗之妻

EMILIA 爱米利娅：伊阿古之妻

BIANCA 比恩卡：凯西奥的情妇

元老、水手、吏役、军官、使者、乐工、传令官、侍从等

地点

第一幕在威尼斯；其余各幕在塞浦路斯岛海口一市镇。

Contents 目录

ACT Ⅰ 第一幕

SCENE I

Venice. A street.
Enter RODERIGO and IAGO.

RODERIGO Tush! never tell me; I take it much unkindly That thou, Iago, who hast had my purse As if the strings were thine, shouldst know of this.

IAGO 'Sblood, but you will not hear me:
If ever I did dream of such a matter, Abhor me.

RODERIGO Thou told'st me thou didst hold him in thy hate.

IAGO Despise me, if I do not. Three great ones of the city,
In personal suit to make me his lieutenant,
Off-capp'd to him: and, by the faith of man,
I know my price, I am worth no worse a place:
But he; as loving his own pride and purposes,
Evades them, with a bombast circumstance
Horribly stuff'd with epithets of war;
And, in conclusion,
Nonsuits my mediators; for, 'Certes,' says he,
'I have already chose my officer.'
And what was he?
Forsooth, a great arithmetician,
One Michael Cassio, a Florentine,
A fellow almost damn'd in a fair wife;
That never set a squadron in the field,
Nor the division of a battle knows
More than a spinster; unless the bookish theoric,
Wherein the toged consuls can propose
As masterly as he: mere prattle, without practise,
Is all his soldiership. But he, sir, had the election:
And I, of whom his eyes had seen the proof

第一场

威尼斯。街道。

罗德利哥及伊阿古上。

罗德利哥 嘿！别对我说，伊阿古；我把我的钱袋交给你支配，让你随意花用，你却做了他们的同谋，这太不够朋友啦。

伊阿古 他妈的！你总不肯听我说下去。要是我做梦会想到这种事情，你不要把我当作一个人。

罗德利哥 你告诉我你恨他。

伊阿古 要是我不恨他，你从此别理我。这城里的三个当道要人亲自向他打招呼，举荐我做他的副将；凭良心说，我知道我自己的价值，难道我就做不得一个副将？可是他眼睛里只有自己没有别人，对于他们的请求，都用一套充满了军事上口头禅的空话回绝了；因为，他说，“我已经选定我的将佐了。”他选中的是个什么人呢？哼，一个算学大家，一个叫作迈克尔·凯西奥的弗罗棱萨人，一个几乎因为娶了娇妻而误了终身的家伙；他从来不曾在战场上领过一队兵，对于布阵作战的知识，懂得简直也不比一个老守空闺的女人多；即使懂得一些书本上的理论，那些身穿宽袍的元老大人们讲起来也会比他更头头是道。只有空谈，不切实际，这就是他的全部的军人资格。可是，老兄，他居然得到了任命；我在罗得斯岛、塞浦路斯岛，以及其他基督徒和异教徒的国土之上，立过多少的军功，都是他亲眼看见的，现在却必须低首下心，受一个市侩的指挥。这位掌柜居然做起他的副将来，而我呢——上帝恕我这样说——却只在这位黑将军的麾下充一名旗官。

At Rhodes, at Cyprus and on other grounds
Christian and heathen, must be be-lee'd and calm'd
By debitor and creditor: this counter-caster,
He, in good time, must his lieutenant be,
And I—God bless the mark!—his Moorship's ancient.

RODERIGO By heaven, I rather would have been his hangman.

IAGO Why, there's no remedy; 'tis the curse of service,
Preferment goes by letter and affection,
And not by old gradation, where each second
Stood heir to the first. Now, sir, be judge yourself,
Whether I in any just term am affined
To love the Moor.

RODERIGO I would not follow him then.

IAGO O, sir, content you;
I follow him to serve my turn upon him:
We cannot all be masters, nor all masters
Cannot be truly follow'd. You shall mark
Many a duteous and knee-crooking knave,
That, doting on his own obsequious bondage,
Wears out his time, much like his master's ass,
For nought but provender, and when he's old, cashier'd:
Whip me such honest knaves. Others there are
Who, trimm'd in forms and visages of duty,
Keep yet their hearts attending on themselves,
And, throwing but shows of service on their lords,
Do well thrive by them and when they have lined their coats
Do themselves homage: these fellows have some soul;
And such a one do I profess myself. For, sir,
It is as sure as you are Roderigo,
Were I the Moor, I would not be Iago:
In following him, I follow but myself;
Heaven is my judge, not I for love and duty,

罗德利哥 天哪，我宁愿做他的刽子手。

伊阿古 这也是没有办法呀。说来真叫人恼恨，军队里的升迁可以全然不管古来的定法，按照各人的阶级依次递补，只要谁的脚力大，能够得到上官的欢心，就可以越级躐升。现在，老兄，请你替我评一评，我究竟有什么理由要跟这摩尔人要好。

罗德利哥 假如是我，我就不愿跟随他。

伊阿古 啊，老兄，你放心吧；我之所以跟随他，不过是要利用他达到我自己的目的。我们不能每个人都是主人，每个主人也不是都该让仆人忠心地追随他。你可以看到，有一辈天生的奴才，他们卑躬屈节，拼命讨主人的好，甘心受主人的鞭策，像一头驴子似的，为了一些粮草而出卖他们的一生，等到年纪老了，主人就把他们撵走；这种老实的奴才是应该抽一顿鞭子的。还有一种人，表面上尽管装出一副鞠躬如也的样子，骨子里却是为他们自己打算；看上去好像替主人做事，实际却靠着主人发展自己的势力，等捞足了油水，就可以知道他所尊敬的其实是他本人；像这种人还有几分头脑；我承认我自己就属于这一类。因为，老兄，正像你是罗德利哥而不是别人一样，我要是做了那摩尔人，我就不会是伊阿古。同样地没有错，虽说我跟随他，其实还是跟随我自己。上天是我的公证人，我这样对他赔着小心，既不是为了忠心，也不是为了义务，只是为了自己的利益，才装出这一副假脸。要是我表面上的恭而敬之的行为会泄露我内心的活动，那么不久我就要掬出我的心来，让乌鸦们乱啄了。世人所知道的我，并不是实在的我。

But seeming so, for my peculiar end:
For when my outward action doth demonstrate
The native act and figure of my heart
In compliment extern, 'tis not long after
But I will wear my heart upon my sleeve
For daws to peck at: I am not what I am.

RODERIGO What a full fortune does the thick-lips owe
If he can carry't thus!

IAGO Call up her father,
Rouse him: make after him, poison his delight,
Proclaim him in the streets; incense her kinsmen,
And, though he in a fertile climate dwell,
Plague him with flies: though that his joy be joy,
Yet throw such changes of vexation on't,
As it may lose some colour.

RODERIGO Here is her father's house; I'll call aloud.

IAGO Do, with like timorous accent and dire yell
As when, by night and negligence, the fire
Is spied in populous cities.

RODERIGO What, ho, Brabantio! Signior Brabantio, ho!

IAGO Awake! what, ho, Brabantio! thieves! thieves! thieves!
Look to your house, your daughter and your bags!
Thieves! thieves!

BRABANTIO appears above, at a window

BRABANTIO What is the reason of this terrible summons?
What is the matter there?

RODERIGO Signior, is all your family within?

IAGO Are your doors lock'd?

BRABANTIO Why, wherefore ask you this?

IAGO 'Zounds, sir, you're robb'd; for shame, put on your gown;
Your heart is burst, you have lost half your soul;

罗德利哥 要是那厚嘴唇的家伙也有这么一手，那可让他交上大运了！

伊 阿 古 叫起她的父亲来；不要放过他，打断他的兴致，在各处街道上宣布他的罪恶；激怒她的亲族。让他虽然住在气候宜人的地方，也免不了受蚊蝇的滋扰，虽然享受着盛大的欢乐，也免不了受烦恼的缠绕。

罗德利哥 这儿就是她父亲的家，我要高声叫喊。

伊 阿 古 很好，你嚷起来吧，就像在一座人口众多的城里，因为晚间失慎而起火的时候，人们用那种惊骇惶恐的声音呼喊一样。

罗德利哥 喂，喂，勃拉班修！勃拉班修先生，喂！

伊 阿 古 醒来！喂，喂！勃拉班修！捉贼！捉贼！捉贼！留心你的屋子、你的女儿和你的钱袋！捉贼！捉贼！

勃拉班修 勃拉班修自上方窗口上。

勃拉班修 大惊小怪地叫什么呀？出了什么事？

罗德利哥 先生，您家里的人没有缺少吗？

伊 阿 古 您的门都锁上了吗？

勃拉班修 咦，你们为什么这样问我？

伊 阿 古 哼！先生，有人偷了您的东西去啦，还不赶快披上您的袍子！您的心碎了，您的灵魂已经丢掉半个；就在这时候，就在这一刻工

Even now, now, very now, an old black ram
Is topping your white ewe. Arise, arise;
Awake the snorting citizens with the bell,
Or else the devil will make a grandsire of you:
Arise, I say.

BRABANTIO What, have you lost your wits?

RODERIGO Most reverend signior, do you know my voice?

BRABANTIO Not I what are you?

RODERIGO My name is Roderigo.

BRABANTIO The worser welcome:
I have charged thee not to haunt about my doors:
In honest plainness thou hast heard me say
My daughter is not for thee; and now, in madness,
Being full of supper and distempering draughts,
Upon malicious bravery, dost thou come
To start my quiet.

RODERIGO Sir, sir, sir,—

BRABANTIO But thou must needs be sure
My spirit and my place have in them power
To make this bitter to thee.

RODERIGO Patience, good sir.

BRABANTIO What tell'st thou me of robbing? this is Venice;
My house is not a grange.

RODERIGO Most grave Brabantio,
In simple and pure soul I come to you.

IAGO 'Zounds, sir, you are one of those that will not
serve God, if the devil bid you. Because we come to do you
service and you think we are ruffians, you'll
have your daughter covered with a Barbary horse;
you'll have your nephews neigh to you; you'll have
coursers for cousins and gennets for germans.

BRABANTIO What profane wretch art thou?

夫，一头老黑羊在跟您的白母羊交尾哩。起来，起来！打钟惊醒那些鼾睡的市民，否则魔鬼要让您抱外孙啦。喂，起来！

勃拉班修 什么！你发疯了吗？

罗德利哥 最可敬的老先生，您听得出我的声音吗？

勃拉班修 我听不出，你是谁？

罗德利哥 我的名字是罗德利哥。

勃拉班修 讨厌！我叫你不要在我的门前走动；我已经老老实实、明明白白对你说，我的女儿是不能嫁给你的；现在你吃饱了饭，喝醉了酒，疯疯癫癫，不怀好意，又要来扰乱我的安静了。

罗德利哥 先生，先生，先生！——

勃拉班修 可是你必须明白，我不是一个好说话的人，要是你惹我发火，凭着我的地位，只要略微拿出一点力量来，你就要叫苦不迭了。

罗德利哥 好先生，不要生气。

勃拉班修 说什么有贼没有贼？这儿是威尼斯，我的屋子不是一座独家的田庄。

罗德利哥 最尊严的勃拉班修，我是一片诚心来通知您。

伊 阿 古 嘿，先生，您也是那种因为魔鬼叫他敬奉上帝而把上帝丢在一旁的人。您把我们当作了坏人，所以把我们的好心看成了恶意，宁愿让您的女儿给一头黑马骑了，替您生下一些马子马孙，攀一些马亲马眷。

勃拉班修 你是个什么混账东西，敢这样胡说八道？

IAGO I am one, sir, that comes to tell you your daughter
and the Moor are now making the beast with two backs.

BRABANTIO Thou art a villain.

IAGO You are—a senator.

BRABANTIO This thou shalt answer; I know thee, Roderigo.

RODERIGO Sir, I will answer any thing. But, I beseech you,
If't be your pleasure and most wise consent,
As partly I find it is, that your fair daughter,
At this odd-even and dull watch o' the night,
Transported, with no worse nor better guard
But with a knave of common hire, a gondolier,
To the gross clasps of a lascivious Moor—
If this be known to you and your allowance,
We then have done you bold and saucy wrongs;
But if you know not this, my manners tell me
We have your wrong rebuke. Do not believe
That, from the sense of all civility,
I thus would play and trifle with your reverence:
Your daughter, if you have not given her leave,
I say again, hath made a gross revolt;
Tying her duty, beauty, wit and fortunes
In an extravagant and wheeling stranger
Of here and every where. Straight satisfy yourself:
If she be in her chamber or your house,
Let loose on me the justice of the state
For thus deluding you.

BRABANTIO Strike on the tinder, ho!
Give me a taper! call up all my people!
This accident is not unlike my dream:
Belief of it oppresses me already.
Light, I say! light!

伊阿古 先生，我是一个特意来告诉您一个消息的人，您的令媛现在正在跟那摩尔人干那件禽兽一样的勾当哩。

勃拉班修 你是个混蛋！

伊阿古 您是一位——元老呢。

勃拉班修 你留点儿神吧，罗德利哥，我认识你。

罗德利哥 先生，我愿意负一切责任，可是请您允许我说一句话。要是令爱因为得到您的明智的同意，所以才会在这样更深人静的午夜，身边并没有一个人保护，让一个下贱的谁都可以雇用的船夫，把她载到一个贪淫的摩尔人的粗野的怀抱里——要是您对于这件事情不但知道，而且默许——照我看来，您至少已经给了她一部分的同意——那么我们的确太放肆、太冒昧了；可是假如您果真不知道这件事，那么从礼貌上说起来，您可不应该对我们恶声相向。难道我会这样一点不懂规矩，敢来戏侮像您这样一位年尊的长者吗？我再说一句，要是令爱没有得到您的许可，就把她的责任、美貌、智慧和财产，全部委弃在一个到处为家、漂泊流浪的异邦人的身上，那么她的确已经干下了一件重大的逆行了。您可以立刻去调查一个明白，要是她好好地在她的房间里或是在您的宅子里，那么是我欺骗了您，您可以按照国法惩办我。

勃拉班修 喂，点起火来！给我一支蜡烛！把我的仆人全都叫起来！这件事情很像我的噩梦，它的极大的可能性已经重压在我的心头了。喂，拿火来！拿火来！

Exit above.

IAGO Farewell; for I must leave you:
It seems not meet, nor wholesome to my place,
To be produced—as, if I stay, I shall—
Against the Moor: for, I do know, the state,
However this may gall him with some cheque,
Cannot with safety cast him, for he's embark'd
With such loud reason to the Cyprus wars,
Which even now stand in act, that, for their souls,
Another of his fathom they have none,
To lead their business: in which regard,
Though I do hate him as I do hell-pains.
Yet, for necessity of present life,
I must show out a flag and sign of love,
Which is indeed but sign.
That you shall surely find him,
Lead to the Sagittary the raised search;
And there will I be with him. So, farewell.

Exit.

Enter, below, BRABANTIO, and Servants with torches.

BRABANTIO It is too true an evil: gone she is;
And what's to come of my despised time
Is nought but bitterness. Now, Roderigo,
Where didst thou see her? O unhappy girl!
With the Moor, say'st thou? Who would be a father!
How didst thou know 'twas she? O she deceives me
Past thought! What said she to you?
Get more tapers:
Raise all my kindred. Are they married, think you?

RODERIGO Truly, I think they are.

自上方下。

伊 阿 古 再会，我要少陪了，要是我不去，我就要出面跟这摩尔人作对证，那不但不大相宜，而且在我的地位上也有很多不便。因为我知道无论他将要因此而受到什么谴责，政府方面现在还不能就把他免职；塞浦路斯的战事正在进行，情势那么紧急，要不是马上派他前去，他们休想找到第二个人有像他那样的才能，可以担当这一个重任。所以虽然我恨他像恨地狱里的刑罚一样，可是为了事实上的必要，我不得不和他假意周旋，那也不过是表面上的敷衍而已。你等他们出来找人的时候，只要领他们到马人旅馆去，一定可以找到他；我也在那边跟他在一起。再见。

下。

勃拉班修率众仆持火炬自下方上。

勃拉班修 真有这样的祸事！她去了；只有悲哀怨恨伴着我这衰朽的余年！罗德利哥，你在什么地方看见她的？——啊，不幸的孩子！——你说跟那摩尔人在一起吗？——谁还愿意做一个父亲！——你怎么知道是她？——唉，想不到她会这样欺骗我！——她对你怎么说？——再拿些蜡烛来！唤醒我的所有的亲族！——你想他们有没有结婚？

罗德利哥 说老实话，我想他们已经结了婚啦。

BRABANTIO O heaven! How got she out?
O treason of the blood!
Fathers, from hence trust not your daughters' minds
By what you see them act. Is there not charms
By which the property of youth and maidhood
May be abused? Have you not read, Roderigo,
Of some such thing?

RODERIGO Yes, sir, I have indeed.

BRABANTIO Call up my brother. O, would you had had her!
Some one way, some another. Do you know
Where we may apprehend her and the Moor?

RODERIGO I think I can discover him, if you please,
To get good guard and go along with me.

BRABANTIO Pray you, lead on. At every house I'll call;
I may command at most. Get weapons, ho!
And raise some special officers of night.
On, good Roderigo: I'll deserve your pains.

Exeunt.

勃拉班修 天哪！她怎么出去的？啊，骨肉的叛逆！做父亲的人啊，从此以后，你们千万留心你们女儿的行动，不要信任她们的心思。世上有没有一种引诱青年少女失去贞操的邪术？罗德利哥，你有没有在书上读到过这一类的事情？

罗德利哥 是的，先生，我的确读到过。

勃拉班修 叫起我的兄弟来！唉，我后悔不让你娶了她去！你们快去给我分头找寻！你知道我们可以在什么地方把她和那摩尔人一起捉到？

罗德利哥 我想我可以找到他的踪迹，要是您愿意多派几个得力的人手跟我前去。

勃拉班修 请你带路。我要到每一个人家去搜寻；大部分的人家都在我的势力之下。喂，多带一些武器！叫起几个巡夜的警吏！去，好罗德利哥，我一定重谢你的辛苦。

同下。

SCENE Ⅱ

Another street.
Enter OTHELLO, IAGO, and Attendants with torches.

IAGO Though in the trade of war I have slain men,
Yet do I hold it very stuff o' the conscience
To do no contrived murder: I lack iniquity
Sometimes to do me service: nine or ten times
I had thought to have yerk'd him here under the ribs.

OTHELLO 'Tis better as it is.

IAGO Nay, but he prated,
And spoke such scurvy and provoking terms
Against your honour
That, with the little godliness I have,
I did full hard forbear him. But, I pray you, sir,
Are you fast married? Be assured of this,
That the magnifico is much beloved,
And hath in his effect a voice potential
As double as the duke's: he will divorce you;
Or put upon you what restraint and grievance
The law, with all his might to enforce it on,
Will give him cable.

OTHELLO Let him do his spite:
My services which I have done the signiory
Shall out-tongue his complaints.
'Tis yet to know,—
Which, when I know that boasting is an honour,
I shall promulgate—I fetch my life and being
From men of royal siege, and my demerits
May speak unbonneted to as proud a fortune
As this that I have reach'd: for know, Iago,
But that I love the gentle Desdemona,
I would not my unhoused free condition

第二场

另一街道。

奥瑟罗、伊阿古及侍从等持火炬上。

伊阿古　虽然我在战场上杀过不少的人，可是总觉得有意杀人是违反良心的；缺少作恶的本能，往往使我不能做我所要做的事。好多次我想要把我的剑从他的肋骨下面刺进去。

奥瑟罗　还是随他说去吧。

伊阿古　可是他唠唠叨叨地说了许多难听的话破坏您的名誉，连像我这样一个荒唐的家伙也实在压不住心头的怒火。可是请问主帅，你们有没有完成婚礼？您要注意，这位元老是很得人心的，他的潜势力比公爵还要大上一倍；他会拆散你们的姻缘，尽量运用法律的力量来给您种种压制和迫害。

奥瑟罗　随他怎样发泄他的愤恨吧；我对贵族们所立的功劳，就可以驳倒他的控诉。世人还没有知道——要是夸口是一件荣耀的事，我就要到处宣布——我是高贵的祖先的后裔，我有充分的资格，享受我目前所得到的值得骄傲的幸运。告诉你吧，伊阿古，倘不是我真心恋爱温柔的苔丝狄蒙娜，即使给我大海中所有的珍宝，我也不愿意放弃我的无拘无束的自由生活，来俯就家室的羁缚的。可是瞧！那边举着火把走来的是些什么人？

Put into circumscription and confine
For the sea's worth.
But, look! what lights come yond?

IAGO Those are the raised father and his friends:
You were best go in.

OTHELLO Not I; I must be found:
My parts, my title and my perfect soul
Shall manifest me rightly. Is it they?

IAGO By Janus, I think no.

Enter CASSIO, and certain Officers with torches.

OTHELLO The servants of the duke, and my lieutenant.
The goodness of the night upon you, friends!
What is the news?

CASSIO The duke does greet you, general,
And he requires your haste-post-haste appearance,
Even on the instant.

OTHELLO What is the matter, think you?

CASSIO Something from Cyprus as I may divine:
It is a business of some heat: the galleys
Have sent a dozen sequent messengers
This very night at one another's heels,
And many of the consuls, raised and met,
Are at the duke's already: you have been hotly call'd for;
When, being not at your lodging to be found,
The senate hath sent about three several guests To search you out.

OTHELLO 'Tis well I am found by you.
I will but spend a word here in the house,and go with you.

Exit.

CASSIO Ancient, what makes he here?

IAGO 'Faith, he tonight hath boarded a land carack:

伊 阿 古 她的父亲带着他的亲友来找您了，您还是进去躲一躲吧。

奥 瑟 罗 不，我要让他们看见我。我的人品、我的地位和我的清白的人格可以替我表明一切。是不是他们？

伊 阿 古 凭二脸神起誓，我想不是。

凯西奥及若干吏役持火炬上。

奥 瑟 罗 原来是公爵手下的人，还有我的副将。晚安，各位朋友！有什么消息？

凯 西 奥 主帅，公爵向您致意，请您立刻就过去。

奥 瑟 罗 你知道是为了什么事？

凯 西 奥 照我猜想起来，大概是塞浦路斯方面的事情，看样子很是紧急。就在这一个晚上，战船上已经连续不断派了十二个使者赶来告急；许多元老都从睡梦中被人叫醒，在公爵府里集合了。他们正在到处找您；因为您不在家里，所以元老院派了三队人出来分头寻访。

奥 瑟 罗 幸而我给你找到了。让我到这儿屋子里去说一句话，就来跟你同去。

下。

凯 西 奥 他到这儿来有什么事？

伊 阿 古 不瞒你说，他今天夜里登上了一艘陆地上的大船，要是能

If it prove lawful prize, he's made for ever.

CASSIO I do not understand.

IAGO He's married.

CASSIO To who?

Re-enter OTHELLO.

IAGO Marry, to—Come, captain, will you go?

OTHELLO Have with you.

CASSIO Here comes another troop to seek for you.

IAGO It is Brabantio. General, be advised;
He comes to bad intent.

Enter BRABANTIO, RODERIGO, and Officers with torches and weapons.

OTHELLO Holla! stand there!

RODERIGO Signior, it is the Moor.

BRABANTIO Down with him, thief!

They draw on both sides.

IAGO You, Roderigo! come, sir, I am for you.

OTHELLO Keep up your bright swords, for the dew will rust them.
Good signior, you shall more command with years
Than with your weapons.

BRABANTIO O thou foul thief, where hast thou stow'd my daughter?
Damn'd as thou art, thou hast enchanted her;
For I'll refer me to all things of sense,
If she in chains of magic were not bound,
Whether a maid so tender, fair and happy,
So opposite to marriage that she shunned
The wealthy curled darlings of our nation,
Would ever have, to incur a general mock,
Run from her guardage to the sooty bosom
Of such a thing as thou, to fear, not to delight.
Judge me the world, if 'tis not gross in sense

够证明那是一件合法的战利品，他可以从此成家立业了。

凯西奥 我不懂你的话。

伊阿古 他结了婚啦。

凯西奥 跟谁结婚？

奥瑟罗重上。

伊阿古 呃，跟——来，主帅，我们走吧。

奥瑟罗 好，我跟你走。

凯西奥 又有一队人来找您了。

伊阿古 那是勃拉班修。主帅，请您留心点儿；他来是不怀好意的。

勃拉班修、罗德利哥及吏役等持火炬武器上。

奥瑟罗 喂！站住！

罗德利哥 先生，这就是那摩尔人。

勃拉班修 杀死他，这贼！

双方拔剑。

伊阿古 你，罗德利哥！来，我们来比个高下。

奥瑟罗 收起你们明晃晃的剑，它们沾了露水会生锈的。老先生，像您这么年高德劭的人，有什么话不可以命令我们，何必动起武来呢？

勃拉班修 啊，你这恶贼！你把我的女儿藏到什么地方去了？你不想想你自己是个什么东西，胆敢用妖法蛊惑她。我们只要凭着情理判断，像她这样一个年轻貌美、娇生惯养的姑娘，多少我们国里有财有势的俊秀子弟她都看不上眼，倘不是中了魔，怎么会不怕人家的笑话，背着尊亲投奔到你这个丑恶的黑鬼的怀里？——那还不早把她吓坏了，岂有什么乐趣可言！世人可以替我评一评，是不是显而易见你用邪恶的符咒欺诱她的娇弱的心灵，用药饵丹方迷惑她的知觉；我要在法庭上叫大家评一评理，这种事情是不是很可能的。所以我现在逮捕你：妨害风化、行使邪术，便是你的罪名。抓住他，要是他敢反抗，你们就用武力制伏他。

That thou hast practised on her with foul charms,
Abused her delicate youth with drugs or minerals
That weaken motion: I'll have't disputed on;
'Tis probable and palpable to thinking.
I therefore apprehend and do attach thee
For an abuser of the world, a practiser
Of arts inhibited and out of warrant.
Lay hold upon him: if he do resist,
Subdue him at his peril.

OTHELLO Hold your hands,
Both you of my inclining, and the rest:
Were it my cue to fight, I should have known it
Without a prompter. Where will you that I go
To answer this your charge?

BRABANTIO To prison, till fit time
Of law and course of direct session
Call thee to answer.

OTHELLO What if I do obey?
How may the duke be therewith satisfied,
Whose messengers are here about my side,
Upon some present business of the state
To bring me to him?

First Officer 'Tis true, most worthy signior;
The duke's in council and your noble self,
I am sure, is sent for.

BRABANTIO How! the duke in council!
In this time of the night! Bring him away:
Mine's not an idle cause: the duke himself,
Or any of my brothers of the state,
Cannot but feel this wrong as 'twere their own;
For if such actions may have passage free,
Bond-slaves and pagans shall our statesmen be.

Exeunt.

奥瑟罗　帮助我的，反对我的，大家放下你们的手！我要是想打架，我自己会知道应该在什么时候动手。您要我到什么地方去答复您的控诉？

勃拉班修　到监牢里去，等法庭上传唤你的时候你再开口。

奥瑟罗　要是我听从您的话去了，那么怎么答复公爵呢？他的使者就在我的身边，因为有紧急的公事，等候着带我去见他。

吏　役　真的，大人，公爵正在举行会议，我相信他已经派人请您去了。

勃拉班修　怎么！公爵在举行会议！在这样夜深的时候！把他带去。我的事情也不是一件等闲小事；公爵和我的同僚们听见了这个消息，一定会感到这种侮辱简直就像加在他们自己身上一般。要是这样的行为可以置之不问，奴隶和异教徒都要来主持我们的国政了。

同下。

SCENE III

A council-chamber.
The DUKE and Senators sitting at a table; Officers attending.

DUKE OF VENICE

There is no composition in these news
That gives them credit.

First Senator Indeed, they are disproportion'd;
My letters say a hundred and seven galleys.

DUKE OF VENICE

And mine, a hundred and forty.

Second Senator And mine, two hundred:
But though they jump not on a just account,—
As in these cases, where the aim reports,
'Tis oft with difference—yet do they all confirm
A Turkish fleet, and bearing up to Cyprus.

DUKE OF VENICE

Nay, it is possible enough to judgment:
I do not so secure me in the error,
But the main article I do approve
In fearful sense.

Sailor *[Within]* What, ho! what, ho! what, ho!

First Officer A messenger from the galleys.

Enter a Sailor.

DUKE OF VENICE

Now, what's the business?

Sailor The Turkish preparation makes for Rhodes;
So was I bid report here to the state
By Signior Angelo.

DUKE OF VENICE

How say you by this change?

第三场

议事厅。

公爵及众元老围桌而坐；吏役等随侍。

公　爵　这些消息彼此分歧，令人难于置信。

元老甲　它们真是参差不一。我的信上说是共有船只一百零七艘。

公　爵　我的信上说是一百四十艘。

元老乙　我的信上又说是二百艘。可是它们所报的数目虽然各个不同，因为根据估计所得的结果，难免多少有些出入，不过它们都证实确有一支土耳其舰队在向塞浦路斯岛进发。

公　爵　嗯，这种事情推想起来很有可能；即使消息不尽正确，我也并不就此放心，大体上总是有根据的，我们倒不能不担着几分心事。

水　手　（在内）喂！喂！喂！有人吗？

吏　役　一个从船上来的使者。

一水手上。

公　爵　什么事？

水　手　安哲鲁大人叫我来此禀告殿下，土耳其人调集舰队，正在向罗得斯岛进发。

公　爵　你们对于这一个变动有什么意见？

First Senator This cannot be,
By no assay of reason: 'tis a pageant,
To keep us in false gaze. When we consider
The importancy of Cyprus to the Turk,
And let ourselves again but understand,
That as it more concerns the Turk than Rhodes,
So may he with more facile question bear it,
For that it stands not in such warlike brace,
But altogether lacks the abilities
That Rhodes is dress'd in: if we make thought of this,
We must not think the Turk is so unskilful
To leave that latest which concerns him first,
Neglecting an attempt of ease and gain,
To wake and wage a danger profitless.

DUKE OF VENICE
Nay, in all confidence, he's not for Rhodes.

First Officer Here is more news.

Enter a Messenger.

Messenger The Ottomites, reverend and gracious,
Steering with due course towards the isle of Rhodes,
Have there injointed them with an after fleet.

First Senator Ay, so I thought. How many, as you guess?

Messenger Of thirty sail: and now they do re-stem
Their backward course, bearing with frank appearance
Their purposes toward Cyprus. Signior Montano,
Your trusty and most valiant servitor,
With his free duty recommends you thus,
And prays you to believe him.

DUKE OF VENICE
'Tis certain, then, for Cyprus.

元老甲　照常识判断起来，这是不会有的事；它无非是转移我们目标的一种诡计。我们只要想一想塞浦路斯岛对于土耳其人的重要性，远在罗得斯岛以上，而且攻击塞浦路斯岛，也比攻击罗得斯岛容易得多，因为它的防务比较空虚，不像罗得斯岛那样戒备严密。我们只要想到这一点，就可以断定土耳其人决不会那样愚笨，甘心舍本逐末，避轻就重，进行一场无益的冒险。

公　爵　嗯，他们的目标决不是罗得斯岛，这是可以断定的。

吏　役　又有消息来了。

一使者上。

使　者　公爵和各位大人，向罗得斯岛驶去的土耳其舰队，已经和另外一支殿后的舰队会合了。

元老甲　嗯，果然符合我的预料。照你猜想起来，一共有多少船只？

使　者　三十艘模样；它们现在已经回过头来，显然是要开向塞浦路斯岛去的。蒙太诺大人，您的忠实英勇的仆人，本着他的职责，叫我来向您报告这一个您可以相信的消息。

公　爵　那么一定是到塞浦路斯岛去的了。玛克斯·勒西科斯不在威尼斯吗？

Marcus Luccicos, is not he in town?

First Senator He's now in Florence.

DUKE OF VENICE

Write from us to him; post-post-haste dispatch.

First Senator Here comes Brabantio and the valiant Moor.

Enter BRABANTIO, OTHELLO, IAGO, RODERIGO, and Officers.

DUKE OF VENICE

Valiant Othello, we must straight employ you
Against the general enemy Ottoman.

To BRABANTIO.

I did not see you; welcome, gentle signior;
We lack'd your counsel and your help tonight.

BRABANTIO So did I yours. Good your grace, pardon me;
Neither my place nor aught I heard of business
Hath raised me from my bed, nor doth the general care
Take hold on me, for my particular grief
Is of so flood-gate and o'erbearing nature
That it engluts and swallows other sorrows
And it is still itself.

DUKE OF VENICE

Why, what's the matter?

BRABANTIO My daughter! O, my daughter!

DUKE OF VENICE

Senator Dead?

BRABANTIO Ay, to me;
She is abused, stol'n from me, and corrupted
By spells and medicines bought of mountebanks;
For nature so preposterously to err,
Being not deficient, blind, or lame of sense,

元老甲　他现在到弗罗棱萨去了。

公　爵　替我写一封十万火急的信给他。

元老甲　勃拉班修和那勇敢的摩尔人来了。

勃拉班修、奥瑟罗、伊阿古、罗德利哥及吏役等上。

公　爵　英勇的奥瑟罗，我们必须立刻派你出去向我们的公敌土耳其人作战。

向勃拉班修。

我没有看见你，欢迎，高贵的大人，我们今晚正需要你的指教和帮助呢。

勃拉班修　我也同样需要您的指教和帮助。殿下，请您原谅，我并不是因为职责所在，也不是因为听到了什么国家大事而从床上惊起；国家的安危不能引起我的注意，因为我个人的悲哀是那么压倒一切，把其余的忧虑一起吞没了。

公　爵　啊，为了什么事？

勃拉班修　我的女儿！啊，我的女儿！

公　爵　众元老，死了吗？

勃拉班修　嗯，她对于我是死了。她已经被人污辱，人家把她从我的地方拐走，用江湖骗子的符咒药物引诱她堕落。因为一个没有残疾、眼睛明亮、理智健全的人，倘不是中了魔法的蛊惑，决不会犯这样荒唐的错误的。

Sans witchcraft could not.

DUKE OF VENICE

Whoe'er he be that in this foul proceeding
Hath thus beguiled your daughter of herself
And you of her, the bloody book of law
You shall yourself read in the bitter letter
After your own sense, yea, though our proper son
Stood in your action.

BRABANTIO Humbly I thank your grace.
Here is the man, this Moor, whom now, it seems,
Your special mandate for the state-affairs
Hath hither brought.

DUKE OF VENICE

Senator We are very sorry for't.

DUKE OF VENICE

[To OTHELLO] What, in your own part, can you say to this?

BRABANTIO Nothing, but this is so.

OTHELLO Most potent, grave, and reverend signiors,
My very noble and approved good masters,
That I have ta'en away this old man's daughter,
It is most true; true, I have married her:
The very head and front of my offending
Hath this extent, no more. Rude am I in my speech,
And little bless'd with the soft phrase of peace:
For since these arms of mine had seven years' pith,
Till now some nine moons wasted, they have used
Their dearest action in the tented field,
And little of this great world can I speak,
More than pertains to feats of broil and battle,
And therefore little shall I grace my cause
In speaking for myself.
Yet, by your gracious patience,

公　爵　如果有人用这种邪恶的手段引诱你的女儿，使她丧失了自己的本性，使你丧失了她，那么无论他是什么人，你都可以根据无情的法律，照你自己的解释给他应得的严刑；即使他是我的儿子，你也可以照样控诉他。

勃拉班修　感谢殿下。罪人就在这儿，就是这个摩尔人；好像您有重要的公事召他来的。

公　爵　众元老，那我们真是抱憾得很。

公　爵　（向奥瑟罗）你自己对于这件事有什么话要分辩？

勃拉班修　没有，事情就是这样。

奥瑟罗　威严无比、德高望重的各位大人，我的尊贵贤良的主人们，我把这位老人家的女儿带走了，这是完全真实的；我已经和她结了婚，这也是真的；我的最大的罪状仅止于此，别的就不是我所知道的了。我的言语是粗鲁的，一点不懂得那些温文尔雅的辞令。因为自从我这双手臂长了七年的膂力以后，直到最近这九个月以前，它们一直都在战场上发挥它们的本领。对于这一个广大的世界，我除了冲锋陷阵以外，几乎一无所知，所以我也不能用什么动人的字句替我自己辩护。可是你们要是愿意耐心听我说下去，我可以向你们讲述一段质朴无文的、关于我的恋爱的全部经过的故事；告诉你们我用什么药物、什么符咒、什么驱神役鬼的手段、什么神奇玄妙的魔法，骗到了他的女儿，因为这是他所控诉我的罪名。

I will a round unvarnish'd tale deliver
Of my whole course of love; what drugs, what charms,
What conjuration and what mighty magic,
For such proceeding I am charged withal,
I won his daughter.

BRABANTIO A maiden never bold;
Of spirit so still and quiet, that her motion
Blush'd at herself; and she, in spite of nature,
Of years, of country, credit, every thing,
To fall in love with what she fear'd to look on!
It is a judgment maim'd and most imperfect
That will confess perfection so could err
Against all rules of nature, and must be driven
To find out practices of cunning hell,
Why this should be. I therefore vouch again
That with some mixtures powerful o'er the blood,
Or with some dram conjured to this effect,
He wrought upon her.

DUKE OF VENICE
To vouch this, is no proof,
Without more wider and more overt test
Than these thin habits and poor likelihoods
Of modern seeming do prefer against him.

First Senator But, Othello, speak:
Did you by indirect and forced courses
Subdue and poison this young maid's affections?
Or came it by request and such fair question
As soul to soul affordeth?

OTHELLO I do beseech you,
Send for the lady to the Sagittary,
And let her speak of me before her father:
If you do find me foul in her report,

勃拉班修 一个素来胆小的女孩子，她的生性是那么幽娴贞静，甚至于心里略为动了一点感情，就会满脸羞愧；像她这样的性质，像她这样的年龄，竟会不顾国族的畛域，把名誉和一切作为牺牲，去跟一个她瞧着都感到害怕的人发生恋爱！假如有人说，这样完美的人儿会做下这样不近情理的事，那这个人的判断可太荒唐了。因此怎么也得查究，到底这里使用了什么样阴谋诡计，才会有这种事情。我断定他一定曾经用烈性的药饵或是邪术炼成的毒剂麻醉了她的血液。

公　爵 没有更确实显明的证据，单单凭着这些表面上的猜测和莫须有的武断，是不能使人信服的。

元老甲 奥瑟罗，你说，你有没有用不正当的诡计诱惑这一位年轻的女郎，或是用强暴的手段逼迫她服从你；还是正大光明地对她披肝沥胆，达到你的求爱的目的？

奥瑟罗 请你们差一个人到马人旅馆去把这位小姐接来，让她当着她的父亲的面告诉你们我是怎样一个人。要是你们根据她的报告，认为我是有罪的，你们不但可以撤销你们对我的信任，解除你们给我的职权，并且可以把我判处死刑。

The trust, the office I do hold of you,
Not only take away, but let your sentence
Even fall upon my life.

DUKE OF VENICE
Fetch Desdemona hither.

OTHELLO Ancient, conduct them: you best know the place.

Exeunt IAGO and Attendants.

And, till she come, as truly as to heaven
I do confess the vices of my blood,
So justly to your grave ears I'll present
How I did thrive in this fair lady's love,
And she in mine.

DUKE OF VENICE
Say it, Othello.

OTHELLO Her father loved me; oft invited me;
Still question'd me the story of my life,
From year to year, the battles, sieges, fortunes,
That I have passed.
I ran it through, even from my boyish days,
To the very moment that he bade me tell it;
Wherein I spake of most disastrous chances,
Of moving accidents by flood and field
Of hair-breadth scapes i' the imminent deadly breach,
Of being taken by the insolent foe
And sold to slavery, of my redemption thence
And portance in my travels' history:
Wherein of antres vast and deserts idle,
Rough quarries, rocks and hills whose heads touch heaven
It was my hint to speak,—such was the process;
And of the Cannibals that each other eat,

公　爵　去把苔丝狄蒙娜带来。

奥瑟罗　旗官，你领他们去，你知道她在什么地方。

伊阿古及吏役等下。

当她没有到来以前，我要像对天忏悔我的血肉的罪恶一样，把我怎样得到这位美人的爱情和她怎样得到我的爱情的经过情形，忠实地向各位陈诉。

公　爵　说吧，奥瑟罗。

奥瑟罗　她的父亲很看重我，常常请我到他家里，每次谈话的时候，总是问起我过去的历史，要我讲述我一年又一年所经历的各次战争、围城和意外的遭遇。我就把我的一生事实，从我的童年时代起，直到他叫我讲述的时候为止，原原本本地说了出来。我说起最可怕的灾祸，海上陆上惊人的奇遇，间不容发的脱险，在傲慢的敌人手中被俘为奴和遇赎脱身的经过，以及旅途中的种种见闻；那些广大的岩窟、荒凉的沙漠、突兀的崖嶂、巍峨的峰岭；接着我又讲到彼此相食的野蛮部落和肩下生头的化外异民；这些都是我的谈话的题目。苔丝狄蒙娜对于这种故事，总是出神倾听。有时为了家庭中的事务，她不能不离座而起，可是她总是尽力把事情赶紧办好，再回来孜孜不倦地把我所讲的每一个字都听了进去。我注意到她这种情形，有一天在一个适当的时间，从她的嘴里逗出了她的真诚的心愿：她希望我能够把我的一生经历，对她作一次详细的复述，因为她平日所听到的，只是一鳞半爪、残缺不全的片段。我答应了她的要求。当我讲到我在少年时代所遭逢的不幸的打击的时候，她往往忍不住掉下泪来。我的故

The Anthropophagi and men whose heads
Do grow beneath their shoulders. This to hear
Would Desdemona seriously incline:
But still the house-affairs would draw her thence:
Which ever as she could with haste dispatch,
She'ld come again, and with a greedy ear
Devour up my discourse: which I observing,
Took once a pliant hour, and found good means
To draw from her a prayer of earnest heart
That I would all my pilgrimage dilate,
Whereof by parcels she had something heard,
But not intentively: I did consent,
And often did beguile her of her tears,
When I did speak of some distressful stroke
That my youth suffer'd. My story being done,
She gave me for my pains a world of sighs:
She swore, in faith, twas strange, 'twas passing strange,
'Twas pitiful, 'twas wondrous pitiful:
She wish'd she had not heard it, yet she wish'd
That heaven had made her such a man: she thank'd me,
And bade me, if I had a friend that loved her,
I should but teach him how to tell my story.
And that would woo her. Upon this hint I spake:
She loved me for the dangers I had pass'd,
And I loved her that she did pity them.
This only is the witchcraft I have used:
Here comes the lady; let her witness it.

Enter DESDEMONA, IAGO, and Attendants.

DUKE OF VENICE

I think this tale would win my daughter too.

事讲完以后，她用无数的叹息酬劳我；她发誓说，那是非常奇异而悲惨的；她希望她没有听到这段故事，可是又希望上天为她造下这样一个男子。她向我道谢，对我说，要是我有一个朋友爱上了她，我只要教他怎样讲述我的故事，就可以得到她的爱情。我听了这一个暗示，才向她吐露我的求婚的诚意。她为了我所经历的种种患难而爱我，我为了她对我所抱的同情而爱她：这就是我的唯一的妖术。她来了，让她为我证明吧。

苔丝狄蒙娜、伊阿古及吏役等上。

公　爵　像这样的故事，我想我的女儿听了也会着迷的。勃拉班修，木已成舟，不必懊恼了。刀剑虽破，比起手无寸铁来，总是略胜

Good Brabantio,
Take up this mangled matter at the best:
Men do their broken weapons rather use
Than their bare hands.

BRABANTIO I pray you, hear her speak:
If she confess that she was half the wooer,
Destruction on my head, if my bad blame
Light on the man! Come hither, gentle mistress:
Do you perceive in all this noble company
Where most you owe obedience?

DESDEMONA My noble father,
I do perceive here a divided duty:
To you I am bound for life and education;
My life and education both do learn me
How to respect you; you are the lord of duty;
I am hitherto your daughter: but here's my husband,
And so much duty as my mother show'd
To you, preferring you before her father,
So much I challenge that I may profess
Due to the Moor my lord.

BRABANTIO God be wi' you! I have done.
Please it your grace, on to the state-affairs:
I had rather to adopt a child than get it.
Come hither, Moor:
I here do give thee that with all my heart
Which, but thou hast already, with all my heart
I would keep from thee. For your sake, jewel,
I am glad at soul I have no other child:
For thy escape would teach me tyranny,
To hang clogs on them. I have done, my lord.

DUKE OF VENICE
Let me speak like yourself, and lay a sentence,

一筹。

勃拉班修 请殿下听她说；要是她承认她本来也有爱慕他的意思，而我却还要归咎于他，那就让我不得好死吧。过来，好姑娘，你看这在座的济济众人之间，谁是你所最应该服从的？

苔丝狄蒙娜 我的尊贵的父亲，我在这里所看到的，是我的分歧的义务：对您说起来，我深荷您的生养教育的大恩，您给我的生命和教养使我明白我应该怎样敬重您；您是我的家长和严君，我直到现在都是您的女儿。可是这儿是我的丈夫，正像我的母亲对您克尽一个妻子的义务，把您看得比她的父亲更重一样，我也应该有权利向这位摩尔人，我的夫主，尽我应尽的名分。

勃拉班修 上帝和你同在！我没有话说了。殿下，请您继续处理国家的要务吧。我宁愿抚养一个义子，也不愿自己生男育女。过来，摩尔人。我现在用我的全副诚心，把她给了你；倘不是你早已得到了她，我一定再也不会让她到你手里。为了你的缘故，宝贝，我很高兴我没有别的儿女，否则你的私奔将要使我变成一个虐待儿女的暴君，替他们手脚加上镣铐。我没有话说了，殿下。

公　爵 让我设身处地，说几句话给你听听，也许可以帮助这一对恋人，使他们能够得到你的欢心。

Which, as a grise or step, may help these lovers
Into your favour.
When remedies are past, the griefs are ended
By seeing the worst, which late on hopes depended.
To mourn a mischief that is past and gone
Is the next way to draw new mischief on.
What cannot be preserved when fortune takes
Patience her injury a mockery makes.
The robb'd that smiles steals something from the thief;
He robs himself that spends a bootless grief.

BRABANTIO So let the Turk of Cyprus us beguile;
We lose it not, so long as we can smile.
He bears the sentence well that nothing bears
But the free comfort which from thence he hears,
But he bears both the sentence and the sorrow
That, to pay grief, must of poor patience borrow.
These sentences, to sugar, or to gall,
Being strong on both sides, are equivocal:
But words are words; I never yet did hear
That the bruised heart was pierced through the ear.
I humbly beseech you, proceed to the affairs of state.

DUKE OF VENICE

The Turk with a most mighty preparation makes for Cyprus. Othello, the fortitude of the place is best known to you; and though we have there a substitute of most allowed sufficiency, yet opinion, a sovereign mistress of effects, throws a more safer voice on you: you must therefore be content to slubber the gloss of your new fortunes with this more stubborn and boisterous expedition.

OTHELLO The tyrant custom, most grave senators,
Hath made the flinty and steel couch of war
My thrice-driven bed of down: I do agnize

眼看希望幻灭，厄运临头，
无可挽回，何必满腹牢愁？
为了既成的灾祸而痛苦，
徒然招惹出更多的灾祸。
既不能和命运争强斗胜，
还是付之一笑，安心耐忍。
聪明人遭盗窃毫不介意；
痛哭流涕反而伤害自己。

勃拉班修 让敌人夺去我们的海岛，
我们同样可以付之一笑。
那感激法官仁慈的囚犯，
他可以忘却刑罚的苦难；
倘然他怨恨那判决太重，
他就要忍受加倍的惨痛。
种种譬解虽能给人慰藉，
它们也会格外添人悲戚；
可是空言毕竟无补实际，
好听的话几曾送进心底？
请殿下继续进行原来的公事吧。

公　爵 土耳其人正在向塞浦路斯大举进犯。奥瑟罗，那岛上的实力你是知道得十分清楚的；虽然我们派在那边代理总督职务的是一个公认为很有能力的人，可是谁都不能不尊重大家的意思，大家觉得由你去负责镇守，才可以万无一失；所以说只得打扰你的新婚的快乐，辛苦你去跑这一趟了。

奥瑟罗 各位尊严的元老们，习惯的暴力已经使我把冷酷无情的战场当作我的温软的眠床，对于艰难困苦，我总是挺身而赴。我愿意接受你们的命令，去和土耳其人作战；可是我要恳求你们念在我替

A natural and prompt alacrity
I find in hardness, and do undertake
These present wars against the Ottomites.
Most humbly therefore bending to your state,
I crave fit disposition for my wife.
Due reference of place and exhibition,
With such accommodation and besort
As levels with her breeding.

DUKE OF VENICE

If you please,
Be't at her father's.

BRABANTIO I'll not have it so.

OTHELLO Nor I.

DESDEMONA Nor I; I would not there reside,
To put my father in impatient thoughts
By being in his eye. Most gracious duke,
To my unfolding lend your prosperous ear;
And let me find a charter in your voice,
To assist my simpleness.

DUKE OF VENICE

What would You, Desdemona?

DESDEMONA That I did love the Moor to live with him,
My downright violence and storm of fortunes
May trumpet to the world: my heart's subdued
Even to the very quality of my lord:
I saw Othello's visage in his mind,
And to his honour and his valiant parts
Did I my soul and fortunes consecrate.
So that, dear lords, if I be left behind,
A moth of peace, and he go to the war,
The rites for which I love him are bereft me,
And I a heavy interim shall support

国家尽心出力，给我的妻子一个适当的安置，按照她的身份，供给她一切日常的需要。

公　爵　你要是同意的话，可以让她住在她父亲的家里。

勃拉班修　我不愿意收留她。

奥瑟罗　我也不能同意。

苔丝狄蒙娜　我也不愿住在父亲的家里，让他每天看见我生气。最仁慈的公爵，愿您俯听我的陈请，让我的卑微的衷忱得到您的谅解和赞助。

公　爵　你有什么请求，苔丝狄蒙娜？

苔丝狄蒙娜　我不顾一切跟命运对抗的行动可以代我向世人宣告，我因为爱这摩尔人，所以愿意和他过共同的生活；我的心灵完全为他的高贵的德性所征服；我先认识他那颗心，然后认识他那奇伟的仪表；我已经把我的灵魂和命运一起呈献给他了。所以，各位大人，要是他一个人迢迢出征，把我遗留在和平的后方，过着像蜉蝣一般的生活，我将要因为不能朝夕侍奉他，而在镂心刻骨的离情别绪中度日如年了。让我跟他去吧。

By his dear absence. Let me go with him.

OTHELLO Let her have your voices.
Vouch with me, heaven, I therefore beg it not,
To please the palate of my appetite,
Nor to comply with heat—the young affects
In me defunct—and proper satisfaction.
But to be free and bounteous to her mind:
And heaven defend your good souls, that you think
I will your serious and great business scant
For she is with me: no, when light-wing'd toys
Of feather'd Cupid seal with wanton dullness
My speculative and offic'd instruments,
That my disports corrupt and taint my business,
Let housewives make a skillet of my helm,
And all indign and base adversities
Make head against my estimation!

DUKE OF VENICE
Be it as you shall privately determine,
Either for her stay or going: the affair cries haste,
And speed must answer it.

First Senator You must away to-night.

OTHELLO With all my heart.

DUKE OF VENICE
At nine i' the morning here we'll meet again.
Othello, leave some officer behind,
And he shall our commission bring to you;
With such things else of quality and respect
As doth import you.

OTHELLO So please your grace, my ancient;
A man he is of honest and trust:
To his conveyance I assign my wife,

奥瑟罗　请你们允许了她吧。上天为我作证，我向你们这样请求，并不是为了贪尝人生的甜头，也不是为了满足我自己的欲望，因为青春的热情在我已成过去了；我的唯一的动机，只是不忍使她失望。请你们千万不要抱着那样的思想，以为她跟我在一起，会使我懈怠了你们所托付给我的重大的使命。不，要是插翅的爱神的风流解数，可以蒙蔽了我的灵明的理智，使我因为贪恋欢娱而误了正事，那么让主妇们把我的战盔当作水罐，让一切的污名都丛集于我的一身吧！

公　爵　她的去留行止，可以由你们自己去决定。事情很是紧急，你必须立刻出发。

元老甲　今天晚上你就得动身。

奥瑟罗　很好。

公　爵　明天早上九点钟，我们还要在这儿聚会一次。奥瑟罗，请你留下一个将佐在这儿，将来政府的委任状好由他转交给你；要是我们随后还有什么决定，可以叫他把训令传达给你。

奥瑟罗　殿下，我的旗官是一个很适当的人物，他的为人是忠实而可靠的；我还要请他负责护送我的妻子，要是此外还有什么必须寄给我的物件，也请殿下一起交给他。

With what else needful your good grace shall think
To be sent after me.

DUKE OF VENICE
Let it be so.
Good night to every one

To BRABANTIO.

And, noble signior,
If virtue no delighted beauty lack,
Your son-in-law is far more fair than black.

First Senator Adieu, brave Moor, use Desdemona well.

BRABANTIO Look to her, Moor, if thou hast eyes to see:
She has deceived her father, and may thee.

Exeunt DUKE OF VENICE, Senators, Officers.

OTHELLO My life upon her faith! Honest Iago,
My Desdemona must I leave to thee:
I prithee, let thy wife attend on her:
And bring them after in the best advantage.
Come, Desdemona: I have but an hour
Of love, of worldly matters and direction,
To spend with thee: we must obey the time.

Exeunt OTHELLO and DESDEMONA.

RODERIGO Iago,—

IAGO What say'st thou, noble heart?

RODERIGO What will I do, think'st thou?

IAGO Why, go to bed, and sleep.

RODERIGO I will incontinently drown myself.

IAGO If thou dost, I shall never love thee after. Why, thou silly gentleman!

公　爵　很好。各位晚安！

向勃拉班修。

尊贵的先生，倘然有德必有貌，说你这位女婿长得黑，远不如说他长得美。

元老甲　再会，勇敢的摩尔人！好好看顾苔丝狄蒙娜。

勃拉班修　留心看着她，摩尔人，不要视而不见；她已经愚弄了她的父亲，她也会把你欺骗。

公爵、众元老、吏役等同下。

奥瑟罗　我用生命保证她的忠诚！正直的伊阿古，我必须把我的苔丝狄蒙娜托付给你，请你叫你的妻子当心照料她；看什么时候有方便，就烦你护送她们起程。来，苔丝狄蒙娜，我只有一小时的工夫和你诉说衷情，料理庶事了。我们必须服从环境的支配。

奥瑟罗、苔丝狄蒙娜同下。

罗德利哥　伊阿古！

伊阿古　你怎么说，好人儿？

罗德利哥　你想我该怎么办？

伊阿古　上床睡觉去吧。

罗德利哥　我立刻就投水去。

伊阿古　好，要是你投了水，我从此不喜欢你了。嘿，你这傻大少爷！

RODERIGO It is silliness to live when to live is torment; and then have we a prescription to die when death is our physician.

IAGO O villainous! I have looked upon the world for four times seven years; and since I could distinguish betwixt a benefit and an injury, I never found man that knew how to love himself. Ere I would say, I would drown myself for the love of a guinea-hen,

I would change my humanity with a baboon.

RODERIGO What should I do? I confess it is my shame to be so fond; but it is not in my virtue to amend it.

IAGO Virtue! a fig! 'tis in ourselves that we are thus or thus. Our bodies are our gardens, to the which our wills are gardeners: so that if we will plant nettles, or sow lettuce, set hyssop and weed up thyme, supply it with one gender of herbs, or distract it with many, either to have it sterile with idleness, or manured with industry, why, the power and corrigible authority of this lies in our wills. If the balance of our lives had not one scale of reason to poise another of sensuality, the blood and baseness of our natures would conduct us to most preposterous conclusions: but we have reason to cool our raging motions, our carnal stings, our unbitted lusts, where of I take this that you call love to be a sect or scion.

RODERIGO It cannot be.

IAGO It is merely a lust of the blood and a permission of the will. Come, be a man. Drown thyself! drown cats and blind puppies. I have professed me thy friend and I confess me knit to thy deserving with cables of perdurable toughness; I could never

better stead thee than now. Put money in thy purse; follow thou the wars; defeat thy favour with an usurped beard; I say, put money in thy purse. It cannot be that Desdemona should long continue her love to the Moor,—put money in thy

罗德利哥 要是活着这样受苦，傻瓜才愿意活下去；一死可以了却烦恼，还是死了的好。

伊阿古 啊，该死！我在这世上也经历过四七二十八个年头了，自从我能够辨别利害以来，我从来不曾看见过什么人知道怎样爱惜他自己。要是我也会为了爱上一个雌儿的缘故而投水自杀，我宁愿变成一头猴子。

罗德利哥 我该怎么办？我承认这样痴心是一件丢脸的事，可是我没有力量把它补救过来呀。

伊阿古 力量！废话！我们变成这样那样，全在于我们自己。我们的身体就像一座园圃，我们的意志是这园圃里的园丁；不论我们插荨麻、种莴苣、栽下牛膝草、拔起百里香，或者单独培植一种草木，或者把全园种得万卉纷披，让它荒废不治也好，把它辛勤耕垦也好，那权力都在于我们的意志。要是在我们的生命之中，理智和情欲不能保持平衡，我们血肉的邪心就会引导我们到一个荒唐的结局；可是我们有的是理智，可以冲淡我们汹涌的热情，肉体的刺激和奔放的淫欲；我认为你所称为“爱情”的，也不过是那样一种东西。

罗德利哥 不，那不是。

伊阿古 那不过是在意志的默许之下一阵情欲的冲动而已。算了，做一个汉子。投水自杀！捉几头大猫小狗投在水里吧！我曾经声明我是你的朋友，我承认我对你的友谊是用不可摧折的、坚韧的缆索联结起来的；现在正是我应该为你出力的时候。把银钱放在你的钱袋里，跟他们出征去；装上一脸假胡子，遮住了你的本来面目——我说，把银钱放在你的钱袋里。苔丝狄蒙娜爱那摩尔人决不会长久——把银钱放在你的钱袋里——他也不会长久爱她。她一开始就把他爱得这样热烈，他们感情的破裂一定也是很突然的——你只要把银钱放在你的钱袋里。这些摩尔人很容易变

purse,—nor he his to her: it was a violent commencement, and thou shalt see an answerable sequestration:—put but money in thy purse. These Moors are changeable in their wills: fill thy purse with money:—the food that to him now is as luscious as locusts, shall be to him shortly as bitter as coloquintida. She must change for youth: when she is sated with his body, she will find the error of her choice: she must have change, she must: therefore put money in thy purse. If thou wilt needs damn thyself, do it a more delicate way than drowning.

Make all the money thou canst: if sanctimony and a frail vow betwixt an erring barbarian and a supersubtle Venetian not too hard for my wits and all the tribe of hell, thou shalt enjoy her; therefore make money. A pox of drowning thyself! it is clean out of the way: seek thou rather to be hanged in compassing thy joy than to be drowned and go without her.

RODERIGO Wilt thou be fast to my hopes, if I depend on the issue?

IAGO Thou art sure of me:—go, make money:—I have told thee often, and I re-tell thee again and again, I hate the Moor: my cause is hearted; thine hath no less reason. Let us be conjunctive in our revenge against him: if thou canst cuckold him, thou dost thyself a pleasure, me a sport. There are many events in the womb of time which will be delivered. Traverse! go, provide thy money. We will have more of this to-morrow. Adieu.

RODERIGO Where shall we meet i' the morning?

IAGO At my lodging.

RODERIGO I'll be with thee betimes.

IAGO Go to; farewell. Do you hear, Roderigo?

RODERIGO What say you?

心——把你的钱袋装满了钱——现在他吃起来像蝗虫一样美味的食物，不久便要变得像苦瓜柯萝辛一样涩口了。她必须换一个年轻的男子；当他的肉体使她餍足了以后，她就会觉悟她的选择的错误。她必须换换口味，她非换不可；所以把银钱放在你的钱袋里。要是你一定要寻死，也得想一个比投水巧妙一点的死法。尽你的力量搜括一些钱。要是凭着我的计谋和魔鬼们的奸诈，破坏这一个走江湖的蛮子和这一个狡猾的威尼斯女人之间的脆弱的盟誓，还不算是一件难事，那么你一定可以享受她——所以快去设法弄些钱来吧。投水自杀！什么话！那根本就不用提；你宁可因为追求你的快乐而被人吊死，总不要在没有一亲她的香泽以前投水自杀。

罗德利哥 要是我指望着这样的好事，你一定会尽力帮助我达到我的愿望吗？

伊 阿 古 你可以完全信任我。去，弄一些钱来。我常常对你说，一次一次反复告诉你，我恨那摩尔人；我的怨毒蓄积在心头，你也对他抱着同样深刻的仇恨，让我们同心合力向他复仇；要是你能够替他戴上一顶绿头巾，你固然是如愿以偿，我也可以拍掌称快。无数人事的变化孕育在时间的胚胎里，我们等着看吧。去，预备好你的钱。我们明天再谈这件事吧。再见。

罗德利哥 明天早上我们在什么地方会面？

伊 阿 古 就在我的寓所里吧。

罗德利哥 我一早就来看你。

伊 阿 古 好，再会。你听见吗，罗德利哥？

罗德利哥 你说什么？

IAGO No more of drowning, do you hear?

RODERIGO I am changed: I'll go sell all my land.

Exit RODERIGO.

IAGO Go to; farewell! put money in your purse.
Thus do I ever make my fool my purse:
For I mine own gain'd knowledge should profane,
If I would time expend with such a snipe.
But for my sport and profit. I hate the Moor:
And it is thought abroad, that 'twixt my sheets
He has done my office: I know not if't be true;
But I, for mere suspicion in that kind,
Will do as if for surety. He holds me well;
The better shall my purpose work on him.
Cassio's a proper man: let me see now:
To get his place and to plume up my will
In double knavery—How, how? Let's see:—
After some time, to abuse Othello's ear
That he is too familiar with his wife.
He hath a person and a smooth dispose
To be suspected, framed to make women false.
The Moor is of a free and open nature,
That thinks men honest that but seem to be so,
And will as tenderly be led by the nose
As asses are.
I have't. It is engender'd. Hell and night
Must bring this monstrous birth to the world's light.

Exit.

伊 阿 古 别再提起投水的话了，你听见没有？

罗德利哥 我已经变了一个人了。我要去把我的田地一起变卖。

罗德利哥下。

伊 阿 古 好，再会！多往你的钱袋里放些钱。我总是这样让这种傻瓜掏出钱来给我花用；因为倘不是为了替自己解解闷，打算占些便宜，那我浪费时间跟这样一个呆子周旋，那才冤枉哩，那还算得什么有见识的人。我恨那摩尔人；有人说他和我的妻子私通，我不知道这句话是真是假；可是在这种事情上，即使不过是嫌疑，我也要把它当作实有其事一样看待。他对我很有好感，这样可以使我对他实行我的计策的时候格外方便一些。凯西奥是一个俊美的男子；让我想想看：夺到他的位置，实现我的一举两得的阴谋；怎么办？怎么办？让我看：等过了一些时候，在奥瑟罗的耳边捏造一些鬼话，说他跟他的妻子看上去太亲热了；他长得漂亮，性情又温和，天生一种媚惑妇人的魔力，像他这种人是很容易引起疑心的。那摩尔人是一个坦白爽直的人，他看见人家在表面上装出一副忠厚诚实的样子，就以为一定是个好人；我可以把他像一头驴子一般牵着鼻子跑。有了！我的计策已经产生。地狱和黑夜正酝酿成这空前的罪恶，它必须向世界显露它的面目。

下。

ACT Ⅱ 第二幕

SCENE I

A Sea-port in Cyprus. An open place near the quay.
Enter MONTANO and two Gentlemen.

MONTANO What from the cape can you discern at sea?

First Gentleman
Nothing at all: it is a highwrought flood;
I cannot, 'twixt the heaven and the main,
Descry a sail.

MONTANO Methinks the wind hath spoke aloud at land;
A fuller blast ne'er shook our battlements:
If it hath ruffian'd so upon the sea,
What ribs of oak, when mountains melt on them,
Can hold the mortise? What shall we hear of this?

Second Gentleman
A segregation of the Turkish fleet:
For do but stand upon the foaming shore,
The chidden billow seems to pelt the clouds;
The wind-shak'd surge, with high and monstrous mane,
Seems to cast water on the burning bear,
And quench the guards of the ever-fixed pole:
I never did like molestation view
On the enchafed flood.

MONTANO If that the Turkish fleet
Be not enshelter'd and embay'd, they are drown'd:
It is impossible they bear it out.

Enter a third Gentleman.

Third Gentleman
News, lads! our wars are done.
The desperate tempest hath so bang'd the Turks,

第一场

塞浦路斯岛海口一市镇。码头附近的广场。

蒙太诺及二军官上。

蒙太诺 你从那海岬望出去，看见海里有什么船只没有？

军官甲 一点望不见。波浪很高，在海天之间，我看不见一片船帆。

蒙太诺 风在陆地上吹得也很厉害,从来不曾有这么大的暴风摇撼过我们的雉堞。要是它在海上也这么猖狂，哪一艘橡树造成的船身支持得住山一样的巨涛迎头倒下？我们将要从这场风暴中间听到什么消息呢？

军官乙 土耳其的舰队一定要被风浪冲散了。你只要站在白沫飞溅的海岸上，就可以看见咆哮的汹涛直冲云霄，被狂风卷起的怒浪奔腾山立，好像要把海水浇向光明的大熊星上，熄灭那照耀北极的亘古不移的斗宿一样。我从来没有见过这样可怕的惊涛骇浪。

蒙太诺 要是土耳其舰队没有避进港里，它们一定沉没了。这样的风浪是抵御不了的。

另一军官上。

军官丙 报告消息！咱们的战事已经结束了。土耳其人遭受这场风暴的突击，不得不放弃他们进攻的计划。一艘从威尼斯来的大船一路上看见他们的船只或沉或破，大部分零落不堪。

That their designment halts: a noble ship of Venice
Hath seen a grievous wreck and sufferance
On most part of their fleet.

MONTANO How! is this true?

Third Gentleman

The ship is here put in,
A Veronesa; Michael Cassio,
Lieutenant to the warlike Moor Othello,
Is come on shore: the Moor himself at sea,
And is in full commission here for Cyprus.

MONTANO I am glad on't; 'tis a worthy governor.

Third Gentleman

But this same Cassio, though he speak of comfort
Touching the Turkish loss, yet he looks sadly,
And prays the Moor be safe; for they were parted
With foul and violent tempest.

MONTANO Pray heavens he be;
For I have served him, and the man commands
Like a full soldier. Let's to the seaside, ho!
As well to see the vessel that's come in
As to throw out our eyes for brave Othello,
Even till we make the main and the aerial blue
An indistinct regard.

Third Gentleman

Come, let's do so:
For every minute is expectancy
Of more arrivance.

Enter CASSIO.

CASSIO Thanks, you the valiant of this warlike isle,
That so approve the Moor! O, let the heavens

蒙太诺 啊！这是真的吗？

军官丙 大船已经在这儿进港，是一艘维洛那造的船；迈克尔·凯西奥，那勇武的摩尔人奥瑟罗的副将，已经上岸来了；那摩尔人自己还在海上，他是奉到全权委任，到塞浦路斯这儿来的。

蒙太诺 我很高兴，这是一位很有才能的总督。

军官丙 可是这个凯西奥说起土耳其的损失，虽然兴高采烈，同时却满脸愁容，祈祷着那摩尔人的安全，因为他们是在险恶的大风浪中彼此失散的。

蒙太诺 但愿他平安无恙。因为我曾经在他手下做过事，知道他在治军用兵这方面，的确是一个大将之才。来，让我们到海边去！一方面看看新到的船舶，一方面把我们的眼睛遥望到海天相接的远处，盼候着勇敢的奥瑟罗。

军官丙 来，我们去吧，因为每一分钟都会有更多的人到来。

凯西奥上。

凯西奥 谢谢，你们这座尚武的岛上的各位壮士，因为你们这样褒奖我们的主帅。啊！但愿上天帮助他战胜风浪，因为我是在险恶的波

Give him defence against the elements,
For I have lost us him on a dangerous sea.

MONTANO Is he well shipp'd?

CASSIO His bark is stoutly timber'd, his pilot
Of very expert and approved allowance;
Therefore my hopes, not surfeited to death,
Stand in bold cure.

A cry within 'A sail, a sail, a sail!'
Enter a fourth Gentleman.

CASSIO What noise?

Fourth Gentleman
The town is empty; on the brow o' the sea
Stand ranks of people, and they cry 'A sail!'

CASSIO My hopes do shape him for the governor.

Guns heard.

Second Gentleman
They do discharge their shot of courtesy:
Our friends at least.

CASSIO I pray you, sir, go forth,
And give us truth who 'tis that is arrived.

Second Gentleman
I shall.

Exit.

MONTANO But, good lieutenant, is your general wiv'd?

CASSIO Most fortunately: he hath achieved a maid
That paragons description and wild fame;
One that excels the quirks of blazoning pens,
And in the essential vesture of creation

涛之中和他失散的。

蒙太诺 他的船靠得住吗？

凯西奥 船身很坚固，舵师是一个大家公认的很有经验的人，所以我还抱着很大的希望。

内呼声："一条船！一条船！一条船！"

一使者上。

凯西奥 什么声音？

使　者 全市的人都出来了，海边站满了人，他们在嚷，"一条船！一条船！"

凯西奥 我希望那就是我们新任的总督。

炮声。

军官乙 他们在放礼炮了；即使不是总督，至少也是我们的朋友。

凯西奥 请你去看一看，回来告诉我们究竟是什么人来了。

军官乙 我就去。

下。

蒙太诺 可是，副将，你们主帅有没有结过婚？

凯西奥 他的婚姻是再幸福不过的。他娶到了一位小姐，她的美貌才德，胜过一切的形容和盛大的名誉；笔墨的赞美不能写尽她的好处，没有一句适当的言语可以充分表达她的天赋的优美。

Does tire the ingener.

Re-enter second Gentleman.

CASSIO How now! who has put in?

Second Gentleman
'Tis one Iago, ancient to the general.

CASSIO Has had most favourable and happy speed:
Tempests themselves, high seas, and howling winds,
The gutter'd rocks and congregated sands—
Traitors ensteep'd to clog the guiltless keel,—
As having sense of beauty, do omit
Their mortal natures, letting go safely by
The divine Desdemona.

MONTANO What is she?

CASSIO She that I spake of, our great captain's captain,
Left in the conduct of the bold Iago,
Whose footing here anticipates our thoughts
A se'nnight's speed. Great Jove, Othello guard,
And swell his sail with thine own powerful breath,
That he may bless this bay with his tall ship,
Make love's quick pants in Desdemona's arms,
Give renew'd fire to our extincted spirits
And bring all Cyprus comfort!

Enter DESDEMONA, EMILIA, IAGO, RODERIGO, and ttendants.

CASSIO O, behold,
The riches of the ship is come on shore!
Ye men of Cyprus, let her have your knees.
Hail to thee, lady! and the grace of heaven,
Before, behind thee, and on every hand,
Enwheel thee round!

军官乙重上。

凯西奥 啊！谁到来了？

军官乙 是元帅麾下的一个旗官，名叫伊阿古。

凯西奥 他倒一帆风顺地到了。汹涌的怒涛，咆哮的狂风，埋伏在海底，跟往来的船只作对的礁石沙碛，似乎也懂得爱惜美人，收敛了它们凶恶的本性，让神圣的苔丝狄蒙娜安然通过。

蒙太诺 她是谁？

凯西奥 就是我刚才说起的，我们大帅的主帅。勇敢的伊阿古护送她到这儿来，想不到他们路上走得这么快，比我们的预期还早七天。伟大的乔武啊，保佑奥瑟罗，吹一口你的大力的气息在他的船帆上，让他的高大的桅墙在这儿海港里显现它的雄姿，让他跳动着一颗恋人的心投进了苔丝狄蒙娜的怀里，重新燃起我们奄奄欲绝的精神，使整个塞浦路斯充满了兴奋！

苔丝狄蒙娜、爱米利娅、伊阿古、罗德利哥及侍从等上。

凯西奥 啊！瞧，船上的珍宝到岸上来了。塞浦路斯人啊，向她下跪吧。祝福你，夫人！愿神灵在你前后左右周遭呵护你！

DESDEMONA I thank you, valiant Cassio.
What tidings can you tell me of my lord?

CASSIO He is not yet arrived: nor know I aught
But that he's well and will be shortly here.

DESDEMONA O, but I fear—How lost you company?

CASSIO The great contention of the sea and skies
Parted our fellowship—But, hark! a sail.

Within 'A sail, a sail!' Guns heard.

Second Gentleman
They give their greeting to the citadel;
This likewise is a friend.

CASSIO See for the news.

Exit Gentleman.

Good ancient, you are welcome.

To EMILIA.

Welcome, mistress.
Let it not gall your patience, good Iago,
That I extend my manners; 'tis my breeding
That gives me this bold show of courtesy.

Kissing her.

IAGO Sir, would she give you so much of her lips
As of her tongue she oft bestows on me,
You'll have enough.

DESDEMONA Alas, she has no speech.

IAGO In faith, too much;
I find it still, when I have list to sleep:
Marry, before your ladyship, I grant,

苔丝狄蒙娜 谢谢您，英勇的凯西奥。您知道我丈夫的什么消息吗？

凯西奥 他还没有到来；我只知道他是平安的，大概不久就会到来。

苔丝狄蒙娜 啊！可是我怕——你们怎么会分散的？

凯西奥 天风和海水的猛烈的激战，使我们彼此失散。可是听！有船来了。

内呼声：“一条船！一条船！”炮声。

军官乙 他们向我们城上放礼炮了；到来的也是我们的朋友。

凯西奥 你去探看探看。

军官乙下。向伊阿古。

老总，欢迎！

向爱米利娅。

欢迎，嫂子！请你不要恼怒，好伊阿古，我总得讲究个礼貌，按照我的教养，我就得来这么一个大胆的见面礼。

吻爱米利娅。

伊阿古 老兄，要是她向你掀动她的嘴唇，也像她向我掀动她的舌头一样，那你就要叫苦不迭了。

苔丝狄蒙娜 唉！她又不会多嘴。

伊阿古 真的，她太会多嘴了；每次我想睡觉的时候，总是被她吵得不得安宁。不过，在您夫人的面前，我还要说一句，她有些话是放在心里说的，人家瞧她不开口，她却在心里骂人。

She puts her tongue a little in her heart,
And chides with thinking.

EMILIA You have little cause to say so.

IAGO Come on, come on; you are pictures out of doors,
Bells in your parlors, wild-cats in your kitchens,
Saints m your injuries, devils being offended,
Players in your housewifery, and housewives' in your beds.

DESDEMONA O, fie upon thee, slanderer!

IAGO Nay, it is true, or else I am a Turk:
You rise to play and go to bed to work.

EMILIA You shall not write my praise.

IAGO No, let me not.

DESDEMONA What wouldst thou write of me, if thou shouldst praise me?

IAGO O gentle lady, do not put me to't;
For I am nothing, if not critical.

DESDEMONA Come on assay. There's one gone to the harbour?

IAGO Ay, madam.

DESDEMONA I am not merry; but I do beguile
The thing I am, by seeming otherwise.
Come, how wouldst thou praise me?

IAGO I am about it; but indeed my invention
Comes from my pate as birdlime does from frize;
It plucks out brains and all: but my Muse labours,
And thus she is deliver'd.
If she be fair and wise, fairness and wit,
The one's for use, the other useth it.

DESDEMONA Well praised! How if she be black and witty?

IAGO If she be black, and thereto have a wit,
She'll find a white that shall her blackness fit.

DESDEMONA Worse and worse.

EMILIA How if fair and foolish?

IAGO She never yet was foolish that was fair;

爱米利娅 你没有理由这样冤枉我。

伊 阿 古 得啦，得啦，你们跑出门来像图画，走进房去像响铃，到了灶下像野猫；害人的时候，面子上装得像个圣徒，人家冒犯了你们，你们便活像夜叉；叫你们管家，你们只会一味胡闹，一上床却又十足像个忙碌的主妇。

苔丝狄蒙娜 啊，啐！你这毁谤女人的家伙！

伊 阿 古 不，我说的话儿千真万确，你们起来游戏，上床工作。

爱米利娅 我再也不要你给我编什么赞美诗了。

伊 阿 古 好，不要叫我编。

苔丝狄蒙娜 要是叫你赞美我，你要怎么编法呢？

伊 阿 古 啊，好夫人，别叫我做这件事，因为我的脾气是要吹毛求疵的。

苔丝狄蒙娜 来，试试看。有人到港口去了吗？

伊 阿 古 是，夫人。

苔丝狄蒙娜 我虽然心里愁闷，姑且强作欢容。来，你怎么赞美我？

伊 阿 古 我正在想着呢。可是我的诗情粘在我的脑壳里，用力一挤就会把脑浆一起挤出的。我的诗神可在难产呢——有了——好容易把孩子养出来了：她要是既漂亮又智慧，就不会误用她的娇美。

苔丝狄蒙娜 赞美得好！要是她虽黑丑而聪明呢？

伊 阿 古 她要是虽黑丑却聪明，包她找到一位俊郎君。

苔丝狄蒙娜 不成话。

爱米利娅 要是美貌而愚笨呢？

伊 阿 古 美女人决不是笨冬瓜，蠢煞也会抱个小娃娃。

For even her folly help'd her to an heir.

DESDEMONA These are old fond paradoxes to make fools laugh i' the alehouse. What miserable praise hast thou for her that's foul and foolish?

IAGO There's none so foul and foolish thereunto,
But does foul pranks which fair and wise ones do.

DESDEMONA O heavy ignorance! thou praisest the worst best.
But what praise couldst thou bestow on a deserving
woman indeed, one that, in the authority of her
merit, did justly put on the vouch of very malice itself ?

IAGO She that was ever fair and never proud,
Had tongue at will and yet was never loud,
Never lack'd gold and yet went never gay,
Fled from her wish and yet said 'Now I may,'
She that being anger'd, her revenge being nigh,
Bade her wrong stay and her displeasure fly,
She that in wisdom never was so frail
To change the cod's head for the salmon's tail;
She that could think and ne'er disclose her mind,
See suitors following and not look behind,
She was a wight, if ever such wight were,—

DESDEMONA To do what?

IAGO To suckle fools and chronicle small beer.

DESDEMONA O most lame and impotent conclusion! Do not learn of him, Emilia, though he be thy husband. How say you, Cassio? is he not a most profane and liberal counsellor?

CASSIO He speaks home, madam: You may relish him more in the soldier than in the scholar.

IAGO *[Aside]* He takes her by the palm: ay, well said,
whisper: with as little a web as this will I ensnare as great a fly as Cassio. Ay, smile upon her, do; I will gyve thee in

苔丝狄蒙娜 这些都是在酒店里骗傻瓜们笑笑的古老的歪诗。还有一种又丑又笨的女人，你也能够勉强赞美她两句吗？

伊 阿 古 别嫌她心肠笨相貌丑，
女人的戏法一样拿手。

苔丝狄蒙娜 啊，岂有此理！你把最好的赞美给了最坏的女人。可是对于一个贤惠的女人——就连天生的坏蛋看见她这么好，也不由得对天起誓，说她真是个好女人——你又怎么赞美她呢？

伊 阿 古 她长得美，却从不骄傲，
能说会道，却从不叫嚣；
有的是钱，但从不妖娆；
摆脱欲念，嘴里说“我要！”
她受人气恼，想把仇报，
却平了气，把烦恼打消；
明白懂事，不朝三暮四，
不拿鳕鱼头换鲑鱼翅；[①]
会动脑筋，却闭紧小嘴，
有人盯梢，她头也不回；
要是有这样的女娇娘——

苔丝狄蒙娜 要她干什么呢？

伊 阿 古 去奶傻孩子，去记油盐账。

苔丝狄蒙娜 啊，这可真是最蹩脚、最松劲的收梢！爱米利娅，不要听他的话，虽然他是你的丈夫。你怎么说，凯西奥？他不是一个粗俗的、胡说八道的家伙吗？

凯 西 奥 他说得很直爽，夫人。您要是把他当作一个军人，不把他当作一个文士，您就不会嫌他出言粗俗了。

伊 阿 古 （*旁白*）他捏着她的手心。嗯，交头接耳，好得很。我只要张起这么一个小小的网，就可以捉住像凯西奥这样一只大苍蝇。嗯，对她微笑，很好；我要叫你跌翻在你自己的礼貌中

---

① 鳕鱼头比喻傻瓜；全句意谓：嫁了傻瓜，并不另找漂亮的相好。

thine own courtship.
You say true; 'tis so, indeed: if such tricks as these strip you out of your lieutenantry, it had been better you had not kissed your three fingers so oft, which now again you are most apt to play the sir in. Very good; well kissed! an excellent courtesy! 'tis so, indeed. Yet again your fingers to your lips? would they were clyster-pipes for your sake!

Trumpet within.

The Moor! I know his trumpet.

CASSIO 'Tis truly so.

DESDEMONA Let's meet him and receive him.

CASSIO Lo, where he comes!

Enter OTHELLO and Attendants.

OTHELLO O my fair warrior!

DESDEMONA My dear Othello!

OTHELLO It gives me wonder great as my content
To see you here before me. O my soul's joy!
If after every tempest come such calms,
May the winds blow till they have waken'd death!
And let the labouring bark climb hills of seas
Olympus-high and duck again as low
As hell's from heaven! If it were now to die,
'Twere now to be most happy; for, I fear,
My soul hath her content so absolute
That not another comfort like to this
Succeeds in unknown fate.

DESDEMONA The heavens forbid
But that our loves and comforts should increase,
Even as our days do grow!

间。——您说得对，正是正是。——要是这种鬼殷勤会葬送你的前程，你还是不要老是吻着你的三个指头，表示你的绅士风度吧。很好，吻得不错！绝妙的礼貌！正是正是。又把你的手指放到你的嘴唇上去了吗？让你的手指头变做你的通肠管我才高兴呢。

喇叭声。

主帅来了！我听得出他的喇叭声音。

凯西奥 真的是他。

苔丝狄蒙娜 让我们去迎接他。

凯西奥 瞧！他来了。

奥瑟罗及侍从等上。

奥瑟罗 啊，我的娇美的战士！

苔丝狄蒙娜 我的亲爱的奥瑟罗！

奥瑟罗 看见你比我先到这里，真使我又惊又喜。啊，我的心爱的人！要是每一次暴风雨之后，都有这样和煦的阳光，那么尽管让狂风肆意地吹，把死亡都吹醒了吧！让那辛苦挣扎的船舶爬上一座座如山的高浪，就像从高高的云上堕下幽深的地狱一般，一泻千丈地跌下来吧！要是我现在死去，那才是最幸福的；因为我怕我的灵魂已经尝到了无上的欢乐，此生此世，再也不会有同样令人欣喜的事情了。

苔丝狄蒙娜 但愿上天眷顾，让我们的爱情和欢乐与日俱增！

OTHELLO Amen to that, sweet powers!
I cannot speak enough of this content;
It stops me here; it is too much of joy:
And this, and this, the greatest discords be.

Kissing her.

That e'er our hearts shall make!

IAGO *[Aside]* O, you are well tuned now!
But I'll set down the pegs that make this music,
As honest as I am.

OTHELLO Come, let us to the castle.
News, friends; our wars are done, the Turks are drown'd.
How does my old acquaintance of this isle?
Honey, you shall be well desired in Cyprus;
I have found great love amongst them. O my sweet,
I prattle out of fashion, and I dote
In mine own comforts. I prithee, good Iago,
Go to the bay and disembark my coffers:
Bring thou the master to the citadel;
He is a good one, and his worthiness
Does challenge much respect. Come, Desdemona,
Once more, well met at Cyprus.

Exeunt OTHELLO, DESDEMONA, and Attendants.

IAGO Do thou meet me presently at the harbour. Come hither. If thou be'st valiant,— as, they say, base men being in love have then a nobility in their natures more than is native to them—list me. The lieutenant tonight watches on the court of guard:—first, I must tell thee this—Desdemona is directly in love with him.

RODERIGO With him! why, 'tis not possible.

奥瑟罗　阿门，慈悲的神明！我不能充分说出我心头的快乐；太多的欢喜憋住了我的呼吸。

吻苔丝狄蒙娜。

一个——再来一个——这便是两颗心儿间最大的冲突了。

伊阿古　（旁白）啊，你们现在是琴瑟调和，看我不动声色，就叫你们松了弦线走了音。

奥瑟罗　来，让我们到城堡里去。好消息，朋友们，我们的战事已经结束，土耳其人全都淹死了。我的岛上的旧友，您好？爱人，你在塞浦路斯将要受到众人的宠爱，我觉得他们都是非常热情的。啊，亲爱的，我自己太高兴了，所以会说出这样忘形的话来。好伊阿古，请你到港口去一趟，把我的箱子搬到岸上。带那船长到城堡里来；他是一个很好的家伙，他的才能非常叫人钦佩。来，苔丝狄蒙娜，我们又在塞浦路斯岛团圆了。

除伊阿古、罗德利哥外均下。

伊阿古　你马上就到港口来会我。过来。人家说，爱情可以刺激懦夫，使他鼓起本来所没有的勇气；要是你果然有胆量，请听我说。副将今晚在卫舍守夜。第一我必须告诉你，苔丝狄蒙娜直截了当地跟他发生了恋爱。

罗德利哥　跟他发生了恋爱！那是不会有的事。

IAGO Lay thy finger thus, and let thy soul be instructed. Mark me with what violence she first loved the Moor, but for bragging and telling her fantastical lies: and will she love him still for prating? let not thy discreet heart think it. Her eye must be fed; and what delight shall she have to look on the devil? When the blood is made dull with the act of sport, there should be, again to inflame it and to give satiety a fresh appetite, loveliness in favour, sympathy in years, manners and beauties; all which the Moor is defective in: now, for want of these required conveniences, her delicate tenderness will find itself abused, begin to heave the gorge, disrelish and abhor the Moor; very nature will instruct her in it and compel her to some second choice. Now, sir, this granted,—as it is a most pregnant and unforced position—who stands so eminent in the degree of this fortune as Cassio does? a knave very voluble; no further conscionable than in putting on the mere form of civil and humane seeming, for the better compassing of his salt and most hidden loose affection? why, none; why, none: a slipper and subtle knave, a finder of occasions, that has an eye can stamp and counterfeit advantages, though true advantage never present itself; a devilish knave. Besides, the knave is handsome, young, and hath all those requisites in him that folly and green minds look after: a pestilent complete knave; and the woman hath found him already.

RODERIGO I cannot believe that in her; she's full of most blessed condition.

IAGO Blessed fig's-end! the wine she drinks is made of grapes: if she had been blessed, she would never have loved the Moor. Blessed pudding! Didst thou not see her paddle with the palm of his hand? didst not mark that?

RODERIGO Yes, that I did; but that was but courtesy.

伊 阿 古 闭住你的嘴，好好听我说。你看她当初不过因为这摩尔人向她吹了些法螺，撒下了一些漫天的大谎，她就爱得他那么热烈；难道她会继续爱他，只是为了他的吹牛的本领吗？你是个聪明人，不要以为世上会有这样的事。她的视觉必须得到满足；她能够从魔鬼脸上感到什么佳趣？情欲在一阵兴奋过了以后而渐生厌倦的时候，必须换一换新鲜的口味，方才可以把它重新刺激起来，或者是容貌的漂亮，或者是年龄的相称，或者是举止的风雅，这些都是这摩尔人所欠缺的；她因为在这些必要的方面不能得到满足，一定会觉得她的青春娇艳所托非人，而开始对这摩尔人由失望而憎恨，由憎恨而厌恶，她的天性就会迫令她再作第二次的选择。这种情形是很自然而可能的；要是承认了这一点，试问哪一个人比凯西奥更有享受这一种福分的便利？一个很会讲话的家伙，为了达到他的秘密的淫邪的欲望，他会恬不为意地装出一副殷勤文雅的外表。哼，谁也比不上他；哼，谁也比不上他！一个狡猾阴险的家伙，惯会乘机取利，无孔不钻——钻得进钻不进他才不管呢。一个鬼一样的家伙！而且，这家伙又漂亮，又年轻，凡是可以使无知妇女醉心的条件，他无一不备；一个十足害人的家伙。这女人已经把他勾上了。

罗德利哥 我不能相信，她是一位圣洁的女人。

伊 阿 古 他妈的圣洁！她喝的酒也是用葡萄酿成的；她要是圣洁，她就不会爱这摩尔人了。哼，圣洁！你没有看见她捏他的手心吗？你没有看见吗？

罗德利哥 是的，我看见的，可是那不过是礼貌罢了。

IAGO Lechery, by this hand; an index and obscure prologue to the history of lust and foul thoughts. They met so near with their lips that their breaths embraced together. Villanous thoughts, Roderigo! when these mutualities so marshal the way, hard at hand comes the master and main exercise, the incorporate conclusion, Pish! But, sir, be you ruled by me: I have brought you from Venice. Watch you to-night; for the command, I'll lay't upon you. Cassio knows you not. I'll not be far from you: do you find some occasion to anger Cassio, either by speaking too loud, or tainting his discipline; or from what other course you please, which the time shall more favourably minister.

RODERIGO Well.

IAGO Sir, he is rash and very sudden in choler, and haply may strike at you: provoke him, that he may; for even out of that will I cause these of Cyprus to mutiny; whose qualification shall come into no true taste again but by the displanting of Cassio. So shall you have a shorter journey to your desires by the means I shall then have to prefer them; and the impediment most profitably removed, without the which there were no expectation of our prosperity.

RODERIGO I will do this, if I can bring it to any opportunity.

IAGO I warrant thee. Meet me by and by at the citadel:
I must fetch his necessaries ashore. Farewell.

RODERIGO Adieu.

Exit.

IAGO That Cassio loves her, I do well believe it;
That she loves him, 'tis apt and of great credit:
The Moor, howbeit that I endure him not,
Is of a constant, loving, noble nature,
And I dare think he'll prove to Desdemona

伊 阿 古 我举手为誓，这明明是奸淫！这一段意味深长的楔子，就包括无限淫情欲念的交流。他们的嘴唇那么贴近，他们的呼吸简直互相拥抱了。该死的思想，罗德利哥！这种表面上的亲热一开了端，主要的好戏就会跟着上场，肉体的结合是必然的结论。呸！可是，老兄，你依着我的话做去。我特意把你从威尼斯带来，今晚你去值班守夜，我会给你把命令弄来；凯西奥是不认识你的；我就在离你不远的地方看着你；你见了凯西奥就找一些借口向他挑衅，或者高声辱骂，破坏他的军纪，或者随你的意思用其他无论什么比较适当的方法。

罗德利哥 好。

伊 阿 古 老兄，他是个性情暴躁、易于发怒的人，也许会向你动武。即使他不动武，你也要激怒他和你打起架来。因为借着这一个理由，我就可以在塞浦路斯人中间煽起一场暴动，假如要平息他们的愤怒，除了把凯西奥解职以外没有其他方法。这样你就可以在我的设计协助之下，早日达到你的愿望，你的阻碍也可以从此除去，否则我们的事情是决无成功之望的。

罗德利哥 我愿意这样干，要是我能够找到下手的机会。

伊 阿 古 那我可以向你保证。等会儿在城门口见我。我现在必须去替他把应用物件搬上岸来。再会。

罗德利哥 再会。

下。

伊 阿 古 凯西奥爱她，这一点我是可以充分相信的；她爱凯西奥，这也是一件很自然而可能的事。这摩尔人我虽然气他不过，却有一副坚定、仁爱、正直的性格；我相信他会对苔丝狄蒙娜做一个最多情的丈夫。讲到我自己，我也是爱她的，并不完全出于情欲的冲动——虽然也许我犯的罪名也并不轻一些儿——可是一半是为

A most dear husband. Now, I do love her too;
Not out of absolute lust, though peradventure
I stand accountant for as great a sin,
But partly led to diet my revenge,
For that I do suspect the lusty Moor
Hath leap'd into my seat; the thought whereof
Doth, like a poisonous mineral, gnaw my inwards;
And nothing can or shall content my soul
Till I am even'd with him, wife for wife,
Or failing so, yet that I put the Moor
At least into a jealousy so strong
That judgment cannot cure. Which thing to do,
If this poor trash of Venice, whom I trash
For his quick hunting, stand the putting on,
I'll have our Michael Cassio on the hip,
Abuse him to the Moor in the rank garb—
For I fear Cassio with my night-cap too—
Make the Moor thank me, love me and reward me.
For making him egregiously an ass
And practising upon his peace and quiet
Even to madness. 'Tis here, but yet confused:
Knavery's plain face is never seen tin used.

Exit.

要报复我的仇恨，因为我疑心这好色的摩尔人已经跳上了我的坐骑。这一种思想像毒药一样腐蚀我的肝肠，什么都不能使我心满意足，除非老婆对老婆，在他身上发泄这一口怨气。即使不能做到这一点，我也要叫这摩尔人心里长起根深蒂固的嫉妒来，没有一种理智的药饵可以把它治疗。为了达到这一个目的，我已经利用这威尼斯的蠢货做我的鹰犬；要是他果然听我的嗾使，我就可以抓住我们那位迈克尔·凯西奥的把柄，在这摩尔人面前大大地诽谤他——因为我疑心凯西奥跟我的妻子也是有些暧昧的。这样我可以让这摩尔人感谢我、喜欢我、报答我，因为我叫他做了一头大大的驴子，用诡计捣乱他的平和安宁，使他因气愤而发疯。方针已经决定，前途未可预料；阴谋的面目直到下手才会揭晓。

下。

SCENE II

A street.
Enter a Herald with a proclamation; People following.

Herald It is Othello's pleasure, our noble and valiant general, that, upon certain tidings now arrived, importing the mere perdition of the Turkish fleet, every man put himself into triumph; some to dance, some to make bonfires, each man to what sport and revels his addiction leads him: for, besides these beneficial news, it is the celebration of his nuptial. So much was his pleasure should be proclaimed. All offices are open, and there is full liberty of feasting from this present hour of five till the bell have told eleven. Heaven bless the isle of Cyprus and our noble general Othello!

Exeunt.

第二场

街道。

传令官持告示上；民众随后。

传令官 我们尊贵英勇的元帅奥瑟罗有令，根据最近接到的消息，土耳其舰队已经全军覆没，全体军民听到这一个捷音，理应同声庆祝：跳舞的跳舞，燃放焰火的燃放焰火，每一个人都可以随他自己的高兴尽情欢乐。因为除了这些可喜的消息以外，我们同时还要祝贺我们元帅的新婚。公家的酒窖、伙食房，一律开放。从下午五时起，直到深夜十一时，大家可以纵情饮酒宴乐。上天祝福塞浦路斯岛和我们尊贵的元帅奥瑟罗！

同下。

SCENE Ⅲ

A hall in the castle.
Enter OTHELLO, DESDEMONA, CASSIO, and Attendants.

OTHELLO Good Michael, look you to the guard to-night:
Let's teach ourselves that honourable stop,
Not to outsport discretion.

CASSIO Iago hath direction what to do;
But, notwithstanding, with my personal eye
Will I look to't.

OTHELLO Iago is most honest.
Michael, good night: tomorrow with your earliest
Let me have speech with you.
[To DESDEMONA] Come, my dear love,
The purchase made, the fruits are to ensue;
That profit's yet to come 'tween me and you.
Good night.

Exeunt OTHELLO, DESDEMONA, and Attendants.
Enter IAGO.

CASSIO Welcome, Iago; we must to the watch.

IAGO Not this hour, lieutenant; 'tis not yet ten o' the clock. Our general cast us thus early for the love of his Desdemona; who let us not therefore blame: he hath not yet made wanton the night with her; and she is sport for Jove.

CASSIO She's a most exquisite lady.

IAGO And, I'll warrant her, fun of game.

CASSIO Indeed, she's a most fresh and delicate creature.

IAGO What an eye she has! methinks it sounds a parley of provocation.

CASSIO An inviting eye; and yet methinks right modest.

第三场

城堡中的厅堂。

奥瑟罗、苔丝狄蒙娜、凯西奥及侍从等上。

奥瑟罗 好迈克尔，今天请你留心警备。我们必须随时谨慎，免得因为纵乐无度而肇成意外。

凯西奥 我已经吩咐伊阿古怎样办了，我自己也要亲自督察照看。

奥瑟罗 伊阿古是个忠实可靠的汉子。迈克尔，晚安，明天你一早就来见我，我有话要跟你说。（向苔丝狄蒙娜）来，我的爱人，我们已经把彼此心身互相交换，愿今后花开结果，恩情美满。晚安！

奥瑟罗、苔丝狄蒙娜及侍从等下。

伊阿古上。

凯西奥 欢迎，伊阿古，我们该守夜去了。

伊阿古 时候还早哪，副将，现在还不到十点钟。咱们主帅因为舍不得他的新夫人，所以这么早就打发我们出去；可是我们也怪不得他，他还没有跟她真个销魂，而她这个人，任是天神见了也要动心的。

凯西奥 她是一位人间无比的佳人。

伊阿古 我可以担保她迷男人的一套功夫可好着呢。

凯西奥 她的确是一个娇艳可爱的女郎。

伊阿古 她的眼睛多么迷人！简直在向人挑战。

凯西奥 一双动人的眼睛，可是却有一种端庄贞静的神气。

IAGO And when she speaks, is it not an alarum to love?

CASSIO She is indeed perfection.

IAGO Well, happiness to their sheets! Come, lieutenant, I have a stoup of wine; and here without are a brace of Cyprus gallants that would fain have a measure to the health of black Othello.

CASSIO Not to-night, good Iago: I have very poor and unhappy brains for drinking: I could well wish courtesy would invent some other custom of entertainment.

IAGO O, they are our friends; but one cup:
I'll drink for you.

CASSIO I have drunk but one cup to-night, and that was craftily qualified too, and, behold, what innovation it makes here: I am unfortunate in the infirmity, and dare not task my weakness with any more.

IAGO What, man! 'tis a night of revels: the gallants desire it.

CASSIO Where are they?

IAGO Here at the door; I pray you, call them in.

CASSIO I'll do't; but it dislikes me.

Exit.

IAGO If I can fasten but one cup upon him,
With that which he hath drunk to-night already,
He'll be as full of quarrel and offence
As my young mistress' dog.
Now, my sick fool Roderigo,
Whom love hath turn'd almost the wrong side out,
To Desdemona hath to-night caroused
Potations pottle-deep; and he's to watch:
Three lads of Cyprus, noble swelling spirits,
That hold their honours in a wary distance,
The very elements of this warlike isle,

伊 阿 古 她说话的时候，不就是爱情的警报吗？

凯 西 奥 她真是十全十美。

伊 阿 古 好，愿他们被窝里快乐！来，副将，我还有一瓶酒；外面有两个塞浦路斯的军官，要想为黑将军祝饮一杯。

凯 西 奥 今夜可不能奉陪了，好伊阿古。我一喝了酒，头脑就会糊涂起来。我希望有人能够发明在宾客欢会的时候，用另外一种方法招待他们。

伊 阿 古 啊，他们都是我们的朋友，喝一杯吧——我也可以代你喝。

凯 西 奥 我今晚只喝了一杯，就是那一杯也被我偷偷地冲了些水，可是你看我这张脸，成个什么样子。我知道自己的弱点，实在不敢再多喝了。

伊 阿 古 嗳哟，朋友！这是一个狂欢的良夜，不要让那些军官们扫兴吧。

凯 西 奥 他们在什么地方？

伊 阿 古 就在这儿门外，请你去叫他们进来吧。

凯 西 奥 我去就去，可是我心里是不愿意的。

下。

伊 阿 古 他今晚已经喝过了一些酒，我只要再灌他一杯下去，他就会像小狗一样到处惹是生非。我们那位为情憔悴的傻瓜罗德利哥今晚为了苔丝狄蒙娜也喝了几大杯的酒，我已经派他守夜了。还有三个心性高傲、重视荣誉的塞浦路斯少年，都是这座尚武的岛上数一数二的人物，我也把他们灌得酩酊大醉；他们今晚也是要守夜的。在这一群醉汉中间，我要叫我们这位凯西奥干出一些可以激动这岛上公愤的事来。可是他们来了。要是结果真就像我所梦想的，我这条顺风船儿顺流而下，前程可远大呢。

Have I to-night fluster'd with flowing cups,
And they watch too.
Now, 'mongst this flock of drunkards,
Am I to put our Cassio in some action
That may offend the isle.—But here they come:
If consequence do but approve my dream,
My boat sails freely, both with wind and stream.

Re-enter CASSIO; with him MONTANO and Gentlemen; servants; following with wine.

CASSIO 'Fore God, they have given me a rouse already.

MONTANO Good faith, a little one; not past a pint, as I am a soldier.

IAGO Some wine, ho! *[Sings]*
And let me the canakin clink, clink;
And let me the canakin clink
A soldier's a man;
A life's but a span;
Why, then, let a soldier drink.
Some wine, boys!

CASSIO 'Fore God, an excellent song.

IAGO I learned it in England, where, indeed, they are most potent in potting: your Dane, your German, and your swag-bellied Hollander—Drink, ho!—are nothing to your English.

CASSIO Is your Englishman so expert in his drinking?

IAGO Why, he drinks you, with facility, your Dane dead drunk; he sweats not to overthrow your Almain; he gives your Hollander a vomit, ere the next pottle can be filled.

CASSIO To the health of our general!

MONTANO I am for it, lieutenant; and I'll do you justice.

IAGO O sweet England!

凯西奥率蒙太诺及军官等重上；众仆持酒后随。

凯西奥 上帝可以作证，他们已经灌了我一满杯啦。

蒙太诺 真的，只是小小的一杯，顶多也不过一品脱的分量。我是一个军人，从来不会说谎的。

伊阿古 喂，酒来！（唱）

一瓶一瓶复一瓶，
饮酒击瓶玎珰鸣。
我为军人岂无情，
人命倏忽如烟云，
聊持杯酒遣浮生。
孩子们，酒来！

凯西奥 好一支歌儿！

伊阿古 这一支歌是我在英国学来的。英国人的酒量才厉害呢，什么丹麦人、德国人、大肚子的荷兰人——酒来！——比起英国人来都算不了什么。

凯西奥 英国人果然这样善于喝酒吗？

伊阿古 嘿，他会不动声色地把丹麦人灌得烂醉如泥，面不流汗地把德国人灌得不省人事，还没有倒满下一杯，那荷兰人已经呕吐狼藉了。

凯西奥 祝我们的主帅健康！

蒙太诺 赞成，副将，您喝我也喝。

伊阿古 啊，可爱的英格兰！（唱）

King Stephen was a worthy peer,
His breeches cost him but a crown;
He held them sixpence all too dear,
With that he call'd the tailor lown.
He was a wight of high renown,
And thou art but of low degree:
'Tis pride that pulls the country down;
Then take thine auld cloak about thee.
Some wine, ho!

CASSIO Why, this is a more exquisite song than the other.

IAGO Will you hear't again?

CASSIO No; for I hold him to be unworthy of his place that does those things. Well, God's above all; and there be souls must be saved, and there be souls must not be saved.

IAGO It's true, good lieutenant.

CASSIO For mine own part,—no offence to the general, nor anyman of quality,—I hope to be saved.

IAGO And so do I too, lieutenant.

CASSIO Ay, but, by your leave, not before me; the lieutenant is to be saved before the ancient. Let's have no more of this; let's to our affairs.—Forgive us our sins!—Gentlemen, let's look to our business.

Do not think, gentlemen. I am drunk: this is my ancient; this is my right hand, and this is my left:

I am not drunk now; I can stand well enough, and speak well enough.

All Excellent well.

CASSIO Why, very well then; you must not think then that I am drunk.

Exit.

英明天子斯蒂芬，
做条裤子五百文；
硬说多花钱六个，
就把裁缝骂一顿。
王爷大名天下传，
你这小子是何人？
骄奢虚荣亡了国，
不如旧衣披在身。
喂，酒来！

凯西奥 呃，这支歌比方才唱的那一支更好听了。

伊阿古 你要再听一遍吗？

凯西奥 不，因为我认为他这样地位的人做出这种事来，是有失体统的。好，上帝在我们头上，有的灵魂必须得救，有的灵魂就不能得救。

伊阿古 对了，副将。

凯西奥 讲到我自己——我并没有冒犯我们主帅或是无论哪一位大人物的意思——我是希望能够得救的。

伊阿古 我也这样希望，副将。

凯西奥 嗯，可是，对不起，你不能比我先得救；副将得救了，然后才是旗官得救。咱们别提这种话啦，还是去干我们的公事吧。上帝赦免我们的罪恶！各位先生，我们不要忘记了我们的事情。不要以为我是醉了，各位先生。这是我的旗官；这是我的右手，这是我的左手。我现在并没有醉；我站得很稳，我说话也很清楚。

众人 非常清楚。

凯西奥 那么很好，你们可不要以为我醉了。

下。

MONTANO To the platform, masters; come, let's set the watch.

IAGO You see this fellow that is gone before;
He is a soldier fit to stand by Caesar
And give direction: and do but see his vice;
'Tis to his virtue a just equinox,
The one as long as the other: 'tis pity of him.
I fear the trust Othello puts him in.
On some odd time of his infirmity,
Will shake this island.

MONTANO But is he often thus?

IAGO 'Tis evermore the prologue to his sleep:
He'll watch the horologe a double set,
If drink rock not his cradle.

MONTANO It were well
The general were put in mind of it.
Perhaps he sees it not; or his good nature
Prizes the virtue that appears in Cassio,
And looks not on his evils: is not this true?

Enter RODERIGO.

IAGO *[Aside to him]* How now, Roderigo!
I pray you, after the lieutenant; go.

Exit RODERIGO.

MONTANO And 'tis great pity that the noble Moor
Should hazard such a place as his own second
With one of an ingraft infirmity:
It were an honest action to say
So to the Moor.

IAGO Not I, for this fair island:
I do love Cassio well; and would do much

蒙太诺 各位朋友，来，我们到露台上守望去。

伊阿古 你们看刚才出去的这一个人，讲到指挥三军的才能，他可以和凯撒争一日之雄。可是你们瞧他这一种酗酒的样子，它正好和他的长处互相抵消。我真为他可惜！我怕奥瑟罗对他如此信任，也许有一天会被他误了大事，使全岛大受震动的。

蒙太诺 可是他常常是这样的吗？

伊阿古 他喝醉了酒总要睡觉；要是没有酒替他催眠，他可以一昼夜睡不着觉。

蒙太诺 这种情形应该向元帅提起。也许他没有觉察，也许他秉性仁恕，因为看重凯西奥的才能而忽略了他的短处。这句话对不对？

罗德利哥上。

伊阿古 （向罗德利哥旁白）怎么，罗德利哥！你快追到那副将后面去吧。去！

罗德利哥下。

蒙太诺 这高贵的摩尔人竟会让一个染上这种恶癖的人做他的辅佐，真是一件令人抱憾的事。谁能够老实对他这样说，才是一个正直的汉子。

伊阿古 即使把这一座大好的岛送给我，我也不愿意说；我很爱凯西奥，要是有办法，我愿意尽力帮助他除去这一种恶癖。可是听！什

To cure him of this evil—But, hark! what noise?
[Cry within: 'Help! help!']

Re-enter CASSIO, driving in RODERIGO.

CASSIO You rogue! you rascal!

MONTANO What's the matter, lieutenant?

CASSIO A knave teach me my duty!
I'll beat the knave into a twiggen bottle.

RODERIGO Beat me!

CASSIO Dost thou prate, rogue?

Striking RODERIGO.

MONTANO Nay, good lieutenant;

CASSIO I pray you, sir, hold your hand. Let me go, sir,
Or I'll knock you o'er the mazzard.

MONTANO Come, come, you're drunk.

CASSIO Drunk!

They fight.

IAGO *[Aside to RODERIGO]*
Away, I say; go out, and cry a mutiny.

Exit RODERIGO.

Nay, good lieutenant,—alas, gentlemen;—
Help, ho!—Lieutenant,—sir,—Montano,—sir;
Help, masters!—Here's a goodly watch indeed!

Bell rings.

Who's that which rings the bell?—Diablo, ho!

么声音？

（内呼声：“救命！救命！”）

凯西奥驱罗德利哥重上。

凯西奥　混蛋！狗贼！

蒙太诺　什么事，副将？

凯西奥　一个混蛋竟敢教训起我来！我要把这混蛋打进一只瓶子里去。

罗德利哥　打我！

凯西奥　你还要利嘴吗，狗贼？

打罗德利哥。

蒙太诺　不，副将，请您住手。

凯西奥　放开我，先生，否则我要一拳打到你的头上来了。

蒙太诺　得啦，得啦，你醉了。

凯西奥　醉了！

与蒙太诺斗。

伊阿古　（向罗德利哥旁白）

快走！到外边去高声嚷叫，说是出了乱子啦。

罗德利哥下。

不，副将！天哪，各位！喂，来人！副将！蒙太诺！帮帮忙，各位朋友！这算是守的什么夜呀！

钟鸣。

谁在那儿打钟？该死！全市的人都要起来了。天哪！副将，住

The town will rise: God's will, lieutenant, hold!
You will be shamed for ever.

Re-enter OTHELLO and Attendants.

OTHELLO What is the matter here?

MONTANO 'Zounds, I bleed still; I am hurt to the death.
Faints

OTHELLO Hold, for your lives!

IAGO Hold, ho! Lieutenant,—sir—Montano,—gentlemen, —
Have you forgot all sense of place and duty?
Hold! the general speaks to you; hold, hold, for shame!

OTHELLO Why, how now, ho! from whence ariseth this?
Are we turn'd Turks, and to ourselves do that
Which heaven hath forbid the Ottomites?
For Christian shame, put by this barbarous brawl:
He that stirs next to carve for his own rage
Holds his soul light; he dies upon his motion.
Silence that dreadful bell: it frights the isle
From her propriety. What is the matter, masters?
Honest Iago, that look'st dead with grieving,
Speak, who began this? on thy love, I charge thee.

IAGO I do not know: friends all but now, even now,
In quarter, and in terms like bride and groom
Devesting them for bed; and then, but now—
As if some planet had unwitted men—
Swords out, and tilting one at other's breast,
In opposition bloody. I cannot speak
Any beginning to this peevish odds;
And would in action glorious I had lost
Those legs that brought me to a part of it!

手！你的脸要从此丢尽啦。

奥瑟罗及侍从等重上。

奥瑟罗 这儿出了什么事情？

蒙太诺 他妈的！我的血流个不停；我受了重伤啦。

奥瑟罗 要活命的快住手！

伊阿古 喂，住手，副将！蒙太诺！各位！你们忘记你们的地位和责任了吗？住手！主帅在对你们说话，还不住手！

奥瑟罗 怎么，怎么！为什么闹起来的？难道我们都变成野蛮人了吗？上天不许土耳其人来打我们，我们倒自相残杀起来了吗？为了基督徒的面子，停止这场粗暴的争吵。谁要是一味怄气，再敢动一动，他就是看轻他自己的灵魂，他一举手我就叫他死。叫他们不要打那可怕的钟；它会扰乱岛上的人心。各位，究竟是怎么一回事？正直的伊阿古，瞧你懊恼得脸色惨淡，告诉我，谁开始这场争闹的？凭着你的忠心，老实对我说。

伊阿古 我不知道。刚才还是好好的朋友，像正在宽衣解带的新夫妇一般相亲相爱，一下子就好像受到什么星光的刺激，迷失了他们的本性，大家竟然拔出剑来，向彼此的胸前直刺过去，拼个你死我活了。我说不出这场任性的争吵是怎么开始的；只怪我这双腿不曾在光荣的战阵上失去，那么我也不会踏进这种是非中间了！

OTHELLO How comes it, Michael, you are thus forgot?
CASSIO I pray you, pardon me; I cannot speak.
OTHELLO Worthy Montano, you were wont be civil;
The gravity and stillness of your youth
The world hath noted, and your name is great
In mouths of wisest censure: what's the matter,
That you unlace your reputation thus
And spend your rich opinion for the name
Of a night-brawler? give me answer to it.
MONTANO Worthy Othello, I am hurt to danger:
Your officer, Iago, can inform you,—
While I spare speech, which something now offends me,—
Of all that I do know: nor know I aught
By me that's said or done amiss this night;
Unless self-charity be sometimes a vice,
And to defend ourselves it be a sin
When violence assails us.
OTHELLO Now, by heaven,
My blood begins my safer guides to rule;
And passion, having my best judgment collied,
Assays to lead the way: if I once stir,
Or do but lift this arm, the best of you
Shall sink in my rebuke. Give me to know
How this foul rout began, who set it on;
And he that is approved in this offence,
Though he had twinn'd with me, both at a birth,
Shall lose me. What! in a town of war,
Yet wild, the people's hearts brimful of fear,
To manage private and domestic quarrel,
In night, and on the court and guard of safety!
'Tis monstrous. Iago, who began't?

奥瑟罗 迈克尔，你怎么会这样忘记你自己的身份？

凯西奥 请您原谅我，我没有话可说。

奥瑟罗 尊贵的蒙太诺，您一向是个温文知礼的人，您的少年端庄为举世所钦佩，在贤人君子之间，您有很好的名声；为什么您会这样自贬身价，牺牲您的宝贵的名誉，让人家说您是个在深更半夜里酗酒闹事的家伙？给我一个回答。

蒙太诺 尊贵的奥瑟罗，我伤得很厉害，不能多说话；您的贵部下伊阿古可以告诉您我所知道的一切。其实我也不知道我在今夜说错了什么话或是做错了什么事，除非自重自爱有时会成了过失，在暴力侵凌的时候，自卫是一桩罪恶。

奥瑟罗 苍天在上，我现在可再也遏制不住我的怒气了。我的血气蒙蔽了清明的理性，叫我只知道凭着冲动的感情行事。我只要动一动，或是举一举这一只胳臂，就可以叫你们中间最有本领的人在我的一怒之下丧失了生命。让我知道这一场可耻的骚扰是怎么开始的，谁是最初肇起事端来的人。要是证实了哪一个人是启衅的罪魁，即使他是我的孪生兄弟，我也不能放过他。什么！一个新遭战乱的城市，秩序还没有恢复，人民的心里充满了恐惧，你们却在深更半夜，在全岛治安所系的所在为了私人间的细故争吵起来！岂有此理！伊阿古，谁是肇事的人？

MONTANO If partially affined, or leagued in office,
Thou dost deliver more or less than truth,
Thou art no soldier.

IAGO Touch me not so near:
I had rather have this tongue cut from my mouth
Than it should do offence to Michael Cassio;
Yet, I persuade myself, to speak the truth
Shall nothing wrong him. Thus it is, general.
Montano and myself being in speech,
There comes a fellow crying out for help:
And Cassio following him with determined sword,
To execute upon him. Sir, this gentleman
Steps in to Cassio, and entreats his pause:
Myself the crying fellow did pursue,
Lest by his clamour—as it so fell out—
The town might fall in fright: he, swift of foot,
Outran my purpose; and I return'd the rather
For that I heard the clink and fall of swords,
And Cassio high in oath; which till to-night
I ne'er might say before. When I came back—
For this was brief—I found them close together,
At blow and thrust; even as again they were
When you yourself did part them.
More of this matter cannot I report:
But men are men; the best sometimes forget:
Though Cassio did some little wrong to him,
As men in rage strike those that wish them best,
Yet surely Cassio, I believe, received
From him that fled some strange indignity,
Which patience could not pass.

OTHELLO I know, Iago,
Thy honesty and love doth mince this matter,

蒙太诺 你要是意存偏袒，或是同僚相护，所说的话和事实不尽符合，你就不是个军人。

伊阿古 不要这样逼我，我宁愿割下自己的舌头，也不愿让它说迈克尔·凯西奥的坏话。可是事已如此，我想说老实话也不算对不起他。是这样的，主帅：蒙太诺跟我正在谈话，忽然跑进一个人来高呼救命，后面跟着凯西奥，杀气腾腾地提着剑，好像一定要杀死他才甘心似的；那时候这位先生就挺身前去拦住凯西奥，请他息怒；我自己追赶那个叫喊的人，因为恐怕他在外边大惊小怪，扰乱人心——后来果然不出我所料；可是他跑得快，我追不上，又听见背后刀剑碰撞和凯西奥高声咒骂的声音，所以就回来了；我从来没有听见他这样骂过人；我本来追得不远，一转身就看见他们在这儿你一刀、我一剑地厮杀得难解难分，正像您到来喝开他们的时候一样。我所能报告的就是这几句话。人总是人，圣贤也有错误的时候；一个人在愤怒之中，就是好朋友也会翻脸不认。虽然凯西奥给了他一点小小的伤害，可是我相信凯西奥一定从那逃走的家伙手里受到什么奇耻大辱，所以才会动起那么大的火性来的。

奥瑟罗 伊阿古，我知道你的忠实和义气，你把这件事情轻描淡写，替凯西奥减轻他的罪名。凯西奥，你是我的好朋友，可是从此以后，

Making it light to Cassio. Cassio, I love thee
But never more be officer of mine.

Re-enter DESDEMONA, attended.

OTHELLO Look, if my gentle love be not raised up!
[TO CASSIO]
I'll make thee an example.

DESDEMONA What's the matter?

OTHELLO All's well now, sweeting; come away to bed.
Sir, for your hurts, myself will be your surgeon:
Lead him off.

To MONTANO, who is led off.

Iago, look with care about the town,
And silence those whom this vile brawl distracted.
Come, Desdemona: 'tis the soldiers' life
To have their balmy slumbers waked with strife.

Exeunt all but IAGO and CASSIO.

IAGO What, are you hurt, lieutenant?

CASSIO Ay, past all surgery.

IAGO Marry, heaven forbid!

CASSIO Reputation, reputation, reputation! O, I have lost my reputation! I have lost the immortal part of myself, and what remains is bestial. My reputation, Iago, my reputation!

IAGO As I am an honest man, I thought you had received some bodily wound; there is more sense in that than in reputation. Reputation is an idle and most false imposition: oft got without merit, and lost without deserving: you have lost no reputation at all, unless you repute yourself such a loser. What, man! there are ways to recover the general

你不是我的部属了。

苔丝狄蒙娜率侍从重上。

奥 瑟 罗 瞧！我的温柔的爱人也给你们吵醒了！（向凯西奥）我要拿你做一个榜样。

苔丝狄蒙娜 什么事？

奥 瑟 罗 现在一切都没事了，亲爱的，去睡吧。先生，您受的伤我愿意亲自替您医治。把他扶出去。

侍从扶蒙太诺下。

伊阿古，你去巡视市街，安定安定受惊的人心。来，苔丝狄蒙娜，难圆的是军人的好梦，才合眼又被杀声惊动。

除伊阿古、凯西奥外均下。

伊 阿 古 什么！副将，你受伤了吗？

凯 西 奥 嗯，我的伤是无药可救的了。

伊 阿 古 嗳哟，上天保佑没有这样的事！

凯 西 奥 名誉，名誉，名誉！啊，我的名誉已经一败涂地了！我已经失去我的生命中不死的一部分，留下来的也就跟畜生没有分别了。我的名誉，伊阿古，我的名誉！

伊 阿 古 我是个老实人，我还以为你受到了什么身体上的伤害，那是比名誉的损失痛苦得多的。名誉是一件无聊的骗人的东西！得到它的人未必有什么功德，失去它的人也未必有什么过失。你的名誉仍旧是好端端的，除非你自以为它已经扫地了。嘿，朋友，你要恢复主帅对你的欢心，尽有办法呢。你现在不过一时遭逢他的恼怒；他给你的这一种处分，与其说是表示对你的不满，还不如说

again: you are but now cast in his mood, a punishment more in policy than in malice, even so as one would beat his offenceless dog to affright an imperious lion: sue to him again, and he's yours.

CASSIO I will rather sue to be despised than to deceive so good a commander with so slight, so drunken, and so indiscreet an officer. Drunk? and speak parrot? and squabble? swagger? swear? and discourse fustian with one's own shadow? O thou invisible spirit of wine, if thou hast no name to be known by, let us call thee devil!

IAGO What was he that you followed with your sword? What had he done to you?

CASSIO I know not.

IAGO Is't possible?

CASSIO I remember a mass of things, but nothing distinctly; a quarrel, but nothing wherefore. O God, that men should put an enemy in their mouths to steal away their brains! that we should, with joy, pleasance revel and applause, transform ourselves into beasts!

IAGO Why, but you are now well enough: how came you thus recovered?

CASSIO It hath pleased the devil drunkenness to give place to the devil wrath; one unperfectness shows me another, to make me frankly despise myself.

IAGO Come, you are too severe a moraler: as the time, the place, and the condition of this country stands, I could heartily wish this had not befallen; but, since it is as it is, mend it for your own good.

CASSIO I will ask him for my place again; he shall tell me I am a drunkard! Had I as many mouths as Hydra, such an answer would stop them all. To be now a sensible man, by and by a fool, and presently a beast! O strange! Every inordinate cup

是遮掩世人耳目的政策，正像有人为了吓退一头凶恶的狮子而故意鞭打他的驯良的狗一样。你只要向他恳求恳求，他一定会回心转意的。

凯西奥 我宁愿恳求他唾弃我，也不愿蒙蔽他的聪明，让这样一位贤能的主帅手下有这么一个酗酒放荡的不肖将校。纵饮无度！胡言乱道！吵架！吹牛！赌咒！跟自己的影子说些废话！啊，你空虚缥缈的旨酒的精灵，要是你还没有一个名字，让我们叫你做魔鬼吧！

伊阿古 你提着剑追逐不舍的那个人是谁？他怎么冒犯了你？

凯西奥 我不知道。

伊阿古 你怎么会不知道？

凯西奥 我记得一大堆的事情，可是全都是模模糊糊的；我记得跟人家吵起来，可是不知道为了什么。上帝啊！人们居然会把一个仇敌放进自己的嘴里，让它偷去他们的头脑！我们居然会在欢天喜地之中，把自己变成了畜生！

伊阿古 可是你现在已经很清醒了。你怎么会明白过来的？

凯西奥 气鬼一上了身，酒鬼就自动退让；一件过失引起了第二件过失，简直使我自己也瞧不起自己了。

伊阿古 得啦，你也太认真了。照此时此地的环境说起来，我但愿没有这种事情发生；可是既然事已如此，替自己谋算个好办法吧。

凯西奥 我要向他请求恢复我的原职，他会对我说我是一个酒棍！即使我有一百张嘴，这样一个答复也会把它们一起封住。现在还是一个清清楚楚的人，不一会儿就变成个傻子，然后立刻就变成一头畜生！啊，奇怪！每一杯过量的酒都是魔鬼酿成的毒汁。

is unblessed and the ingredient is a devil.

IAGO Come, come, good wine is a good familiar creature, if it be well used: exclaim no more against it.
And, good lieutenant, I think you think I love you.

CASSIO I have well approved it, sir. I drunk!

IAGO You or any man living may be drunk! at a time, man.
I'll tell you what you shall do. Our general's wife is now the general: may say so in this respect, for that he hath devoted and given up himself to the contemplation, mark, and denotement of her parts and graces: confess yourself freely to her; importune her help to put you in your place again: she is of so free, so kind, so apt, so blessed a disposition, she holds it a vice in her goodness not to do more than she is requested: this broken joint between you and her husband entreat her to splinter; and, my fortunes against any lay worth naming, this crack of your love shall grow stronger than it was before.

CASSIO You advise me well.

IAGO I protest, in the sincerity of love and honest kindness.

CASSIO I think it freely; and betimes in the morning I will beseech the virtuous Desdemona to undertake for me:
I am desperate of my fortunes if they cheque me here.

IAGO You are in the right. Good night, lieutenant; I must to the wach.

CASSIO Good night, honest Iago.

Exit.

IAGO And what's he then that says I play the villain?
When this advice is free I give and honest,
Probal to thinking and indeed the course
To win the Moor again? For 'tis most easy
The inclining Desdemona to subdue
In any honest suit: she's framed as fruitful
As the free elements. And then for her

伊阿古 算了，算了，好酒只要不滥喝，也是一个很好的伙伴，你也不用咒骂它了。副将，我想你一定把我当作一个好朋友看待。

凯西奥 我很信任你的友谊。我醉了！

伊阿古 朋友，一个人有时候多喝了几杯，也是免不了的。让我告诉你一个办法。我们主帅的夫人现在是我们真正的主帅；我可以这样说，因为他心里只念着她的好处，眼睛里只看见她的可爱。你只要在她面前坦白忏悔，恳求恳求她，她一定会帮助你官复原职。她的性情是那么慷慨仁慈，那么体贴人心，人家请她出十分力，她要是没有出到十二分，就觉得好像对不起人似的。你请她替你弥缝弥缝你跟她的丈夫之间的这一道裂痕，我可以拿我的全部财产打赌，你们的交情一定反而会因此格外加强的。

凯西奥 你的主意出得很好。

伊阿古 我发誓这一种意思完全出于一片诚心。

凯西奥 我充分信任你的善意，明天一早我就请求贤德的苔丝狄蒙娜替我尽力说情。要是我在这儿给他们革退了，我的前途也就从此毁了。

伊阿古 你说得对。晚安，副将，我还要守夜去呢。

凯西奥 晚安，正直的伊阿古！

下。

伊阿古 谁说我做事奸恶？我贡献给他的这番意见，不是光明正大、很合理，而且的确是挽回这摩尔人的心意的最好办法吗？只要是正当的请求，苔丝狄蒙娜总是有求必应的；她的为人是再慷慨、再热心不过的了。至于叫她去说动这摩尔人，更是不费吹灰之力；他的灵魂已经完全成为她的爱情的俘虏，无论她要做什么事，或是把已经做成的事重新推翻，即使叫他抛弃他的信仰和一切得救的希望，他也会唯命是从，让她的喜恶主宰他的无力反抗的身心。

To win the Moor—were't to renounce his baptism,
All seals and symbols of redeemed sin,
His soul is so enfetter'd to her love,
That she may make, unmake, do what she list,
Even as her appetite shall play the god
With his weak function. How am I then a villain
To counsel Cassio to this parallel course,
Directly to his good? Divinity of hell!
When devils will the blackest sins put on,
They do suggest at first with heavenly shows,
As I do now: for whiles this honest fool
Plies Desdemona to repair his fortunes
And she for him pleads strongly to the Moor,
I'll pour this pestilence into his ear,
That she repeals him for her body's lust;
And by how much she strives to do him good,
She shall undo her credit with the Moor.
So will I turn her virtue into pitch,
And out of her own goodness make the net
That shall enmesh them all.

Re-enter RODERIGO.

IAGO How now, Roderigo!

RODERIGO I do follow here in the chase, not like a hound that hunts, but one that fills up the cry. My money is almost spent; I have been to-night exceedingly well cudgelled; and I think the issue will be, I shall have so much experience for my pains, and so, with no money at all and a little more wit, return again to Venice.

IAGO How poor are they that have not patience!
What wound did ever heal but by degrees?

我既然凑合着凯西奥的心意，向他指示了这一条对他有利的方策，谁还能说我是个恶人呢？佛面蛇心的鬼魅！恶魔往往用神圣的外表，引诱世人干最恶的罪行，正像我现在所用的手段一样。因为当这个老实的呆子恳求苔丝狄蒙娜为他转圜，当她竭力在那摩尔人面前替他说情的时候，我就要用毒药灌进那摩尔人的耳中，说是她所以要运动凯西奥复职，只是为了恋奸情热的缘故。这样她越是忠于所托，越是会加强那摩尔人的猜疑。我就利用她的善良的心肠污毁她的名誉，让他们一个个都落进了我的罗网之中。

罗德利哥重上。

伊阿古 啊，罗德利哥！

罗德利哥 我跟着大伙儿赶到这儿来，不像一头追寻狐兔的猎狗，倒像是替你们凑凑热闹的。我的钱也差不多花光了，今夜我还挨了一顿痛打；我想这番教训，大概就是我费去不少辛苦换来的代价了。现在我的钱囊已经空空如也，我的头脑里总算增加了一点智慧，我要回威尼斯去了。

伊阿古 没有耐性的人是多么可怜！什么伤口不是慢慢地平复起来的？你知道我们干事情全赖计谋，并不是用的魔法；用计谋就必须等待

Thou know'st we work by wit, and not by witchcraft;
And wit depends on dilatory time.
Does't not go well? Cassio hath beaten thee.
And thou, by that small hurt, hast cashier'd Cassio:
Though other things grow fair against the sun,
Yet fruits that blossom first will first be ripe:
Content thyself awhile. By the mass, 'tis morning;
Pleasure and action make the hours seem short.
Retire thee; go where thou art billeted:
Away, I say; thou shalt know more hereafter:
Nay, get thee gone.

Exit RODERIGO.

Two things are to be done:
My wife must move for Cassio to her mistress;
I'll set her on;
Myself the while to draw the Moor apart,
And bring him jump when he may Cassio find
Soliciting his wife: ay, that's the way
Dull not device by coldness and delay.

Exit.

时机成熟。一切不是进行得很顺利吗？凯西奥固然把你打了一顿，可是你受了一点小小的痛苦，已经使凯西奥把官职都丢了。虽然在太阳光底下，各种草木都欣欣向荣，可是最先开花的果子总是最先成熟。你安心点儿吧。嗳哟，天已经亮啦；又是喝酒，又是打架，闹哄哄的就让时间飞过去了。你去吧，回到你的宿舍里去；去吧，有什么消息我再来告诉你；去吧。

罗德利哥下。

我还要做两件事情：第一是叫我的妻子在她的女主人面前替凯西奥说两句好话；我就去怂恿她；同时我就去设法把那摩尔人骗开，等到凯西奥去向他的妻子请求的时候，再让他亲眼看见这幕把戏。好，言之有理，不要迁延不决，耽误了锦囊妙计。

下。

ACT Ⅲ　第三幕

SCENE I

Cyprus. Before the castle.
Enter CASSIO and some Musicians.

CASSIO Masters, play here; I will content your pains;
Something that's brief; and bid 'Good morrow, general.'

Music.
Enter Clown.

Clown Why masters, have your instruments been in Naples, that they speak i' the nose thus?

First Musician How, sir, how!

Clown Are these, I pray you, wind-instruments?

First Musician Ay, marry, are they, sir.

Clown O, thereby hangs a tail.

First Musician Whereby hangs a tale, sir?

Clown Marry. sir, by many a wind-instrument that I know.
But, masters, here's money for you: and the general so likes your music, that he desires you, for love's sake, to make no more noise with it.

First Musician Well, sir, we will not.

Clown If you have any music that may not be heard, to't again: but, as they say to hear music the general does not greatly care.

First Musician We have none such, sir.

Clown Then put up your pipes in your bag, for I'll away:
go; vanish into air; away!

Exeunt Musicians.

CASSIO Dost thou hear, my honest friend?

Clown No, I hear not your honest friend; I hear you.

CASSIO Prithee, keep up thy quillets. There's a poor piece of gold for

第一场

塞浦路斯。城堡前。

凯西奥及若干乐工上。

凯西奥　列位朋友，就在这儿奏起来吧，我会酬劳你们的。奏一支简短一些的乐曲，敬祝我们的主帅晨安。

音乐。

小丑上。

小　丑　怎么，列位朋友，你们的乐器都曾到过那不勒斯，所以会这样嗡咙嗡咙地用鼻音说话吗？

乐工甲　怎么，大哥，怎么？

小　丑　请问这些都是管乐器吗？

乐工甲　正是，大哥。

小　丑　啊，怪不得下面有个那玩意儿。

乐工甲　怪不得有个什么玩意儿，大哥？

小　丑　我说，有好多管乐器就都是这么回事。可是，列位朋友，这儿是赏给你们的钱；将军非常喜欢你们的音乐，他请求你们千万不要再奏下去了。

乐工甲　好，大哥，我们不奏就是了。

小　丑　要是你们会奏听不见的音乐，请奏起来吧；可是正像人家说的，将军对于听音乐这件事不大感兴趣。

乐工甲　我们不会奏那样的音乐。

小　丑　那么把你们的笛子藏起来，因为我要去了。去，消灭在空气里吧。去！

乐工等下。

凯西奥　你听没听见，我的好朋友？

小　丑　不，我没有听见您的好朋友，我只听见您。

凯西奥　少说笑话。这一块小小的金币你拿了去，要是侍候将军夫人的那

thee: if the gentlewoman that attends the general's wife be stirring, tell her there's one Cassio entreats her a little favour of speech: wilt thou do this?

Clown She is stirring, sir: if she will stir hither, I shall seem to notify unto her.

CASSIO Do, good my friend.

Exit Clown.
Enter IAGO.

CASSIO In happy time, Iago.

IAGO You have not been a-bed, then?

CASSIO Why, no; the day had broke
Before we parted. I have made bold, Iago,
To send in to your wife: my suit to her
Is, that she will to virtuous Desdemona
Procure me some access.

IAGO I'll send her to you presently;
And I'll devise a mean to draw the Moor
Out of the way, that your converse and business
May be more free.

CASSIO I humbly thank you for't.

Exit IAGO.

I never knew
A Florentine more kind and honest.

Enter EMILIA.

EMILIA Good morrow, good Lieutenant: I am sorry
For your displeasure; but all will sure be well.
The general and his wife are talking of it;
And she speaks for you stoutly: the Moor replies,

位奶奶已经起身，你就告诉她有一个凯西奥请她出来说话。你肯不肯？

小　丑　她已经起身了，先生；要是她愿意出来，我就告诉她。

凯西奥　谢谢你，我的好朋友。

小丑下。
伊阿古上。

凯西奥　来得正好，伊阿古。

伊阿古　你还没有上过床吗？

凯西奥　没有，我们分手的时候，天早就亮了。伊阿古，我已经大胆叫人去请你的妻子出来；我想请她替我设法见一见贤德的苔丝狄蒙娜。

伊阿古　我去叫她立刻出来见你。我还要想一个法子把那摩尔人调开，好让你们谈话方便一些。

凯西奥　多谢你的好意。

伊阿古下。

我从来没有认识过一个比他更善良正直的弗罗棱萨人。

爱米利娅上。

爱米利娅　早安，副将！听说您误触主帅之怒，真是一件令人懊恼的事；可是一切就会转祸为福的。将军和他的夫人正在谈起此事，夫人竭力替您辩白，将军说，被您伤害的那个人，在塞浦路斯是很有名誉、很有势力的，为了避免受人非难起见，他不得不把您斥革；

That he you hurt is of great fame in Cyprus,
And great affinity, and that in wholesome wisdom
He might not but refuse you; but he protests he loves you
And needs no other suitor but his likings
To take the safest occasion by the front
To bring you in again.

CASSIO Yet, I beseech you,
If you think fit, or that it may be done,
Give me advantage of some brief discourse
With Desdemona alone.

EMILIA Pray you, come in;
I will bestow you where you shall have time
To speak your bosom freely.

CASSIO I am much bound to you.

Exeunt.

可是他说他很喜欢您，即使没有别人替您说情，他由于喜欢您，也会留心着一有适当的机会，就让您恢复原职的。

凯 西 奥 可是我还要请求您一件事：要是您认为没有妨碍，或是可以办得到的话，请您设法让我独自见一见苔丝狄蒙娜，跟她作一次简短的谈话。

爱米利娅 请您进来吧，我可以带您到一处可以让您从容吐露您的心曲的所在。

凯 西 奥 那真使我感激万分了。

同下。

SCENE II

A room in the castle.
Enter OTHELLO, IAGO, and Gentlemen.

OTHELLO These letters give, Iago, to the pilot;
And by him do my duties to the senate:
That done, I will be walking on the works;
Repair there to me.

IAGO Well, my good lord, I'll do't.

OTHELLO This fortification, gentlemen, shall we see't?

All We'll wait upon your lordship.

Exeunt.

第二场

城堡中一室。

奥瑟罗、伊阿古及军官等上。

奥瑟罗 伊阿古，这几封信你拿去交给舵师，叫他回去替我呈上元老院。我就在堡垒上走走！你把事情办好以后，就到那边来见我。

伊阿古 是，主帅，我就去。

奥瑟罗 各位，我们要不要去看看这儿的防务？

众　人 我们愿意奉陪。

同下。

SCENE III

The garden of the castle.
Enter DESDEMONA, CASSIO, and EMILIA.

DESDEMONA Be thou assured, good Cassio, I will do
All my abilities in thy behalf.

EMILIA Good madam, do: I warrant it grieves my husband,
As if the case were his.

DESDEMONA O, that's an honest fellow. Do not doubt, Cassio,
But I will have my lord and you again
As friendly as you were.

CASSIO Bounteous madam,
Whatever shall become of Michael Cassio,
He's never any thing but your true servant.

DESDEMONA I know't; I thank you. You do love my lord:
You have known him long; and be you well assured
He shall in strangeness stand no further off
Than in a polite distance.

CASSIO Ay, but, lady,
That policy may either last so long,
Or feed upon such nice and waterish diet,
Or breed itself so out of circumstance,
That, I being absent and my place supplied,
My general will forget my love and service.

DESDEMONA Do not doubt that; before Emilia here
I give thee warrant of thy place: assure thee,
If I do vow a friendship, I'll perform it
To the last article: my lord shall never rest;
I'll watch him tame and talk him out of patience;
His bed shall seem a school, his board a shrift;
I'll intermingle every thing he does

第三场

城堡前。

苔丝狄蒙娜、凯西奥及爱米利娅上。

苔丝狄蒙娜 好凯西奥，你放心吧，我一定尽力替你说情就是了。

爱米利娅 好夫人，请您千万出力。不瞒您说，我的丈夫为了这件事情，也懊恼得不得了，就像是他自己身上的事情一般。

苔丝狄蒙娜 啊！你的丈夫是一个好人。放心吧，凯西奥，我一定会设法使我的丈夫对你恢复原来的友谊。

凯 西 奥 大恩大德的夫人，无论迈克尔·凯西奥将来会有什么成就，他永远是您的忠实的仆人。

苔丝狄蒙娜 我知道，我感谢你的好意。你爱我的丈夫，你又是他的多年的知交；放心吧，他除了表面上因为避免嫌疑而对你略示疏远以外，决不会真把你见外的。

凯 西 奥 您说得很对，夫人。可是为了这“避嫌”，时间可能就要拖得很长，或是为了一些什么细碎小事，再三考虑之后还是不便叫我回来，结果我失去了在帐下供奔走的机会，日久之后，有人代替了我的地位，恐怕主帅就要把我的忠诚和微劳一起忘记了。

苔丝狄蒙娜 那你不用担心，当着爱米利娅的面，我保证你一定可以回复原职。请你相信我，要是我发誓帮助一个朋友，我一定会帮助他到底。我的丈夫将要不得安息，无论睡觉吃饭的时候，我都要在他耳旁聒噪；无论他干什么事，我都要插进嘴去替凯西奥说情。所以高兴起来吧，凯西奥，因为你的辩护人是宁死不愿放弃你的权益的。

With Cassio's suit: therefore be merry, Cassio;
For thy solicitor shall rather die
Than give thy cause away.

EMILIA Madam, here comes my lord.

CASSIO Madam, I'll take my leave.

DESDEMONA Why, stay, and hear me speak.

CASSIO Madam, not now: I am very ill at ease,
Unfit for mine own purposes.

DESDEMONA Well, do your discretion.

Exit CASSIO Enter OTHELLO and IAGO.

IAGO Ha! I like not that.

OTHELLO What dost thou say?

IAGO Nothing, my lord: or if—I know not what.

OTHELLO Was not that Cassio parted from my wife?

IAGO Cassio, my lord! No, sure, I cannot think it,
That he would steal away so guilty-like,
Seeing you coming.

OTHELLO I do believe 'twas he.

DESDEMONA How now, my lord!
I have been talking with a suitor here,
A man that languishes in your displeasure.

OTHELLO Who is't you mean?

DESDEMONA Why, your lieutenant, Cassio. Good my lord,
If I have any grace or power to move you,
His present reconciliation take;
For if he be not one that truly loves you,
That errs in ignorance and not in cunning,
I have no judgment in an honest face:
I prithee, call him back.

OTHELLO Went he hence now?

爱米利娅 夫人，将军来了。

凯 西 奥 夫人，我告辞了。

苔丝狄蒙娜 啊，等一等，听我说。

凯 西 奥 夫人，改日再谈吧；我现在心里很不自在，见了主帅恐怕反多不便。

苔丝狄蒙娜 好，随您的便。

凯西奥下。

伊 阿 古 嘿！我不喜欢那种样子。

奥 瑟 罗 你说什么？

伊 阿 古 没有什么，主帅，要是——我不知道。

奥 瑟 罗 那从我妻子身边走开去的，不是凯西奥吗？

伊 阿 古 凯西奥，主帅？不，不会有那样的事，我不能够设想，他一看见您来了，就好像做了什么虚心事似的，偷偷地溜走了。

奥 瑟 罗 我相信是他。

苔丝狄蒙娜 啊，我的主！刚才有人在这儿向我请托，他因为失去了您的欢心，非常抑郁不快呢。

奥 瑟 罗 你说的是什么人？

苔丝狄蒙娜 就是您的副将凯西奥呀。我的好夫君，要是我还有几分面子，或是几分可以左右您的力量，请您立刻对他恢复原来的恩宠吧。因为他倘不是一个真心爱您的人，他的过失倘不是无心而是有意的，那么我就是看错了人啦。请您叫他回来吧。

奥 瑟 罗 他刚才从这儿走开吗？

DESDEMONA Ay, sooth; so humbled
That he hath left part of his grief with me,
To suffer with him. Good love, call him back.

OTHELLO Not now, sweet Desdemona; some other time.

DESDEMONA But shall't be shortly?

OTHELLO The sooner, sweet, for you.

DESDEMONA Shall't be to-night at supper?

OTHELLO No, not to-night.

DESDEMONA To—morrow dinner, then?

OTHELLO I shall not dine at home;
I meet the captains at the citadel.

DESDEMONA Why, then, to-morrow night; or Tuesday morn;
On Tuesday noon, or night; on Wednesday morn:
I prithee, name the time, but let it not
Exceed three days: in faith, he's penitent;
And yet his trespass, in our common reason—
Save that, they say, the wars must make examples
Out of their best—is not almost a fault
To incur a private cheque. When shall he come?
Tell me, Othello: I wonder in my soul,
What you would ask me, that I should deny,
Or stand so mammering on. What! Michael Cassio,
That came a-wooing with you, and so many a time,
When I have spoke of you dispraisingly,
Hath ta'en your part; to have so much to do
To bring him in! Trust me, I could do much,—

OTHELLO Prithee, no more: let him come when he will;
I will deny thee nothing.

DESDEMONA Why, this is not a boon;
'Tis as I should entreat you wear your gloves,
Or feed on nourishing dishes, or keep you warm,
Or sue to you to do a peculiar profit

苔丝狄蒙娜 嗯，是的。他是那样满含着羞愧，使我也不禁对他感到同情的悲哀。爱人，叫他回来吧。

奥瑟罗 现在不必，亲爱的苔丝狄蒙娜，慢慢再说吧。

苔丝狄蒙娜 可是那不会太久吗？

奥瑟罗 亲爱的，为了你的缘故，我叫他早一点复职就是了。

苔丝狄蒙娜 能不能在今天晚餐的时候？

奥瑟罗 不，今晚可不能。

苔丝狄蒙娜 那么明天午餐的时候？

奥瑟罗 明天我不在家里午餐，我要跟将领们在营中会面。

苔丝狄蒙娜 那么明天晚上吧，或者星期二早上，星期二中午，晚上，星期三早上，随您指定一个时间，可是不要超过三天。他对于自己的行为失检，的确非常悔恨。固然在这种战争的时期，听说必须惩办那最好的人物，给全军立个榜样，可是照我们平常的眼光看来，他的过失实在是微乎其微，不必受什么个人的处分。什么时候让他来？告诉我，奥瑟罗。要是您有什么事情要求我，我想我决不会拒绝您，或是这样吞吞吐吐的。什么！迈克尔·凯西奥，您向我求婚的时候，是他陪着您来的；好多次我表示对您不满意的时候，他总是为您辩护；现在我请您把他重新叙用，却会这样为难！相信我，我可以——

奥瑟罗 好了，不要说下去了。让他随便什么时候来吧；你要什么我总不愿拒绝的。

苔丝狄蒙娜 这并不是一个恩惠，就好像我请求您戴上您的手套，劝您吃些富于营养的菜肴，穿些温暖的衣服，或是叫您做一件对您自己有益的事情一样。不，要是我真的向您提出什么要求，来试探试探您的爱情，那一定是一件非常棘手而难以应允的事。

To your own person: nay, when I have a suit
Wherein I mean to touch your love indeed,
It shall be full of poise and difficult weight
And fearful to be granted.

OTHELLO I will deny thee nothing:
Whereon, I do beseech thee, grant me this,
To leave me but a little to myself.

DESDEMONA Shall I deny you? no: farewell, my lord.

OTHELLO Farewell, my Desdemona: I'll come to thee straight.

DESDEMONA Emilia, come. Be as your fancies teach you;
Whate'er you be, I am obedient.

Exeunt DESDEMONA and EMILIA.

OTHELLO Excellent wretch! Perdition catch my soul,
But I do love thee! and when I love thee not,
Chaos is come again.

IAGO My noble lord—

OTHELLO What dost thou say, Iago?

IAGO Did Michael Cassio, when you woo'd my lady,
Know of your love?

OTHELLO He did, from first to last: why dost thou ask?

IAGO But for a satisfaction of my thought;
No further harm.

OTHELLO Why of thy thought, Iago?

IAGO I did not think he had been acquainted with her.

OTHELLO O, yes; and went between us very oft.

IAGO Indeed!

OTHELLO Indeed! ay, indeed: discern'st thou aught in that?
Is he not honest?

IAGO Honest, my lord!

OTHELLO Honest! ay, honest.

奥瑟罗　我什么都不愿拒绝你，可是现在你必须答应暂时离开我一会儿。

苔丝狄蒙娜　我会拒绝您的要求吗？不。再会，我的主。

奥瑟罗　再会，我的苔丝狄蒙娜，我马上就来看你。

苔丝狄蒙娜　爱米利娅，来吧。您爱怎么样就怎么样，我总是服从您的。

苔丝狄蒙娜、爱米利娅同下。

奥瑟罗　可爱的女人！要是我不爱你，愿我的灵魂永堕地狱！当我不爱你的时候，世界也要复归于混沌了。

伊阿古　尊贵的主帅——

奥瑟罗　你说什么，伊阿古？

伊阿古　当您向夫人求婚的时候，迈克尔·凯西奥也知道你们在恋爱吗？

奥瑟罗　他从头到尾都知道。你为什么问起？

伊阿古　不过是为了解释我心头的一个疑惑，并没有其他用意。

奥瑟罗　你有什么疑惑，伊阿古？

伊阿古　我以为他本来跟夫人是不相识的。

奥瑟罗　啊，不，他常常在我们两人之间传递消息。

伊阿古　当真！

奥瑟罗　当真！嗯，当真。你觉得有什么不对吗？他这人不老实吗？

伊阿古　老实，我的主帅？

奥瑟罗　老实！嗯，老实。

IAGO My lord, for aught I know.
OTHELLO What dost thou think?
IAGO Think, my lord!
OTHELLO Think, my lord!
By heaven, he echoes me,
As if there were some monster in his thought
Too hideous to be shown. Thou dost mean something:
I heard thee say even now, thou lik'dst not that,
When Cassio left my wife: what didst not like?
And when I told thee he was of my counsel
In my whole course of wooing, thou criedst, 'Indeed!'
And didst contract and purse thy brow together,
As if thou then hadst shut up in thy brain
Some horrible conceit: if thou dost love me,
Show me thy thought.
IAGO My lord, you know I love you.
OTHELLO I think thou dost;
And, for I know thou'rt full of love and honesty,
And weigh'st thy words before thou giv'st them breath,
Therefore these stops of thine fright me the more:
For such things in a false disloyal knave
Are tricks of custom, but in a man that's just
They are close delations, working from the heart
That passion cannot rule.
IAGO For Michael Cassio,
I dare be sworn I think that he is honest.
OTHELLO I think so too.
IAGO Men should be what they seem;
Or those that be not, would they might seem none!
OTHELLO Certain, men should be what they seem.
IAGO Why, then, I think Cassio's an honest man.
OTHELLO Nay, yet there's more in this:

伊阿古 主帅，照我所知道的——

奥瑟罗 你有什么意见？

伊阿古 意见，我的主帅！

奥瑟罗 意见，我的主帅！天哪，他在学我的舌，好像在他的思想之中，藏着什么丑恶得不可见人的怪物似的。你的话里含着意思。刚才凯西奥离开我的妻子的时候，我听见你说，你不喜欢那种样子,你不喜欢什么样子呢？当我告诉你在我求婚的全部过程中他都参与我们的秘密的时候，你又喊着说，“当真！”蹙紧了你的眉头，好像在把一个可怕的思想锁在你的脑筋里一样。要是你爱我，把你所想到的事告诉我吧。

伊阿古 主帅，您知道我是爱您的。

奥瑟罗 我相信你的话。因为我知道你是一个忠诚正直的人，从来不让一句没有忖度过的话轻易出口，所以你这种吞吞吐吐的口气格外使我惊疑。在一个奸诈的小人，这些不过是一套玩惯了的戏法；可是在一个正人君子，那就是从心底里不知不觉自然流露出来的秘密的抗议。

伊阿古 讲到迈克尔·凯西奥，我敢发誓我相信他是忠实的。

奥瑟罗 我也这样想。

伊阿古 人们的内心应该跟他们的外表一致，有的人却不是这样；要是他们能够脱下了假面，那就好了！

奥瑟罗 不错，人们的内心应该跟他们的外表一致。

伊阿古 所以我想凯西奥是个忠实的人。

奥瑟罗 不，我看你还有一些别的意思。请你老老实实把你心中的意思告

I prithee, speak to me as to thy thinkings,
As thou dost ruminate, and give thy worst of thoughts
The worst of words.

IAGO Good my lord, pardon me:
Though I am bound to every act of duty,
I am not bound to that all slaves are free to.
Utter my thoughts? Why, say they are vile and false;
As where's that palace whereinto foul things
Sometimes intrude not? who has a breast so pure,
But some uncleanly apprehensions
Keep leets and law-days and in session sit
With meditations lawful?

OTHELLO Thou dost conspire against thy friend, Iago,
If thou but think'st him wrong'd and mak'st his ear
A stranger to thy thoughts.

IAGO I do beseech you—
Though I perchance am vicious in my guess,
As, I confess, it is my nature's plague
To spy into abuses, and oft my jealousy
Shapes faults that are not—that your wisdom yet,
From one that so imperfectly conceits,
Would take no notice, nor build yourself a trouble
Out of his scattering and unsure observance.
It were not for your quiet nor your good,
Nor for my manhood, honesty, or wisdom,
To let you know my thoughts.

OTHELLO What dost thou mean?

IAGO Good name in man and woman, dear my lord,
Is the immediate jewel of their souls:
Who steals my purse steals trash; 'tis something, nothing;
'Twas mine, 'tis his, and has been slave to thousands:
But he that filches from me my good name

诉我，尽管用最坏的字眼，说出你所想到的最坏的事情。

伊阿古 我的好主帅，请原谅我；凡是我名分上应尽的责任，我当然不敢躲避，可是您不能勉强我做那一切奴隶们也没有那种义务的事。吐露我的思想？也许它们是邪恶而卑劣的。哪一座庄严的宫殿里，不会有时被下贱的东西闯入呢？哪一个人的心胸这样纯洁，没有一些污秽的念头和正大的思想分庭抗礼呢？

奥瑟罗 伊阿古，要是你以为你的朋友受人欺侮了，可是却不让他知道你的思想，这不成合谋卖友了吗？

伊阿古 也许我是以小人之腹度君子之心，因为——我承认我有一种坏毛病，是个秉性多疑的人，常常会无中生有，错怪了人家，所以请您凭着您的见识，还是不要把我的无稽的猜测放在心上，更不要因为我的胡乱的妄言而自寻烦恼。要是我让您知道了我的思想，一则将会破坏您的安宁，对您没有什么好处；二则那会影响我的人格，对我也是一件不智之举。

奥瑟罗 你的话是什么意思？

伊阿古 我的好主帅，无论男人女人，名誉是他们灵魂里面最切身的珍宝。谁偷窃我的钱囊，不过偷窃到一些废物，一些虚无的东西，它只是从我的手里转到他的手里，而它也曾做过千万人的奴隶。可是谁偷去了我的名誉，那么他虽然并不因此而富足，我却因为失去它而成为赤贫了。

Robs me of that which not enriches him
And makes me poor indeed.

OTHELLO By heaven, I'll know thy thoughts.

IAGO You cannot, if my heart were in your hand;
Nor shall not, whilst 'tis in my custody.

OTHELLO Ha!

IAGO O, beware, my lord, of jealousy;
It is the green-eyed monster which doth mock
The meat it feeds on; that cuckold lives in bliss
Who, certain of his fate, loves not his wronger;
But, O, what damned minutes tells he o'er
Who dotes, yet doubts, suspects, yet strongly loves!

OTHELLO O misery!

IAGO Poor and content is rich and rich enough,
But riches fineless is as poor as winter
To him that ever fears he shall be poor.
Good heaven, the souls of all my tribe defend
From jealousy!

OTHELLO Why, why is this?
Think'st thou I'ld make a lie of jealousy,
To follow still the changes of the moon
With fresh suspicions? No; to be once in doubt
Is once to be resolved: exchange me for a goat,
When I shall turn the business of my soul
To such exsufflicate and blown surmises,
Matching thy inference. 'Tis not to make me jealous
To say my wife is fair, feeds well, loves company,
Is free of speech, sings, plays and dances well;
Where virtue is, these are more virtuous:
Nor from mine own weak merits will I draw
The smallest fear or doubt of her revolt;
For she had eyes, and chose me. No, Iago;

奥瑟罗 凭着上天起誓，我一定要知道你的思想。

伊阿古 即使我的心在您的手里，您也不能知道我的思想；当它还在我的保管之下，我更不能让您知道。

奥瑟罗 嘿！

伊阿古 啊，主帅，您要留心嫉妒啊！那是一个绿眼的妖魔，谁做了它的牺牲，就要受它的玩弄。本来并不爱他的妻子的那种丈夫，虽然明知被他的妻子欺骗，算来还是幸福的。可是啊！一方面那样痴心疼爱，一方面又是那样满腹狐疑，这才是活活的受罪！

奥瑟罗 啊，难堪的痛苦！

伊阿古 贫穷而知足，可以赛过富有；有钱的人要是时时刻刻都在担心他会有一天变成穷人，那么即使他有无限的资财，实际上也像冬天一样贫困。天啊，保佑我们不要嫉妒吧！

奥瑟罗 咦，这是什么意思？你以为我会在嫉妒里消磨我的一生，随着每一次月亮的变化，发生一次新的猜疑吗？不，我有一天感到怀疑，就要把它立刻解决。要是我会让这种捕风捉影的猜测支配我的心灵，像你所暗示的那样，我就是一头愚蠢的山羊。谁说我的妻子貌美多姿，爱好交际，口才敏慧，能歌善舞，弹得一手好琴，决不会使我嫉妒；对于一个贤淑的女子，这些是锦上添花的美妙的外饰。我也绝不因为我自己的缺点而担心她会背叛我；她倘不是独具慧眼，决不会选中我的。不，伊阿古，我在没有亲眼目睹以前，决不妄起猜疑；当我感到怀疑的时候，我就要把它证实；果然有了确实的证据，我就一了百了，让爱情和嫉妒同时毁灭。

I'll see before I doubt; when I doubt, prove;
And on the proof, there is no more but this,—
Away at once with love or jealousy!

IAGO I am glad of it; for now I shall have reason
To show the love and duty that I bear you
With franker spirit: therefore, as I am bound,
Receive it from me. I speak not yet of proof.
Look to your wife; observe her well with Cassio;
Wear your eye thus, not jealous nor secure:
I would not have your free and noble nature,
Out of self-bounty, be abused; look to't:
I know our country disposition well;
In Venice they do let heaven see the pranks
They dare not show their husbands;their best conscience
Is not to leave't undone, but keep't unknown.

OTHELLO Dost thou say so?

IAGO She did deceive her father, marrying you;
And when she seem'd to shake and fear your looks,
She loved them most.

OTHELLO And so she did.

IAGO Why, go to then;
She that, so young, could give out such a seeming,
To seal her father's eyes up close as oak-
He thought 'twas witchcraft—but I am much to blame;
I humbly do beseech you of your pardon
For too much loving you.

OTHELLO I am bound to thee for ever.

IAGO I see this hath a little dash'd your spirits.

OTHELLO Not a jot, not a jot.

IAGO I' faith, I fear it has.
I hope you will consider what is spoke
Comes from my love. But I do see you're moved:

伊阿古 您这番话使我听了很是高兴，因为我现在可以用更坦白的精神，向您披露我的忠爱之忱了；既然我不能不说，您且听我说吧。我还不能给您确实的证据。注意尊夫人的行动；留心观察她对凯西奥的态度；用冷静的眼光看着他们，不要一味多心，也不要过于大意。我不愿您的慷慨豪迈的天性被人欺罔；留心着吧。我知道我们国里娘儿们的脾气；在威尼斯她们背着丈夫干的风流活剧，是不瞒天地的；她们可以不顾羞耻，干她们所要干的事，只要不让丈夫知道，就可以问心无愧。

奥瑟罗 你真的这样说吗？

伊阿古 她当初跟您结婚，曾经骗过她的父亲；当她好像对您的容貌战栗畏惧的时候，她的心里却在热烈地爱着它。

奥瑟罗 她正是这样。

伊阿古 好，她这样小小的年纪，就有这般能耐，做作得不露一丝破绽，把她父亲的眼睛完全遮掩过去，使他疑心您用妖术把她骗走。——可是我不该说这种话；请您原谅我对您的过分的忠心吧。

奥瑟罗 我永远感激你的好意。

伊阿古 我看这件事情有点儿令您扫兴。

奥瑟罗 一点不，一点不。

伊阿古 真的，我怕您在生气啦。我希望您把我这番话当作善意的警戒。可是我看您真的在动怒啦。我必须请求您不要因为我这么说了，就武断地下了结论；不过是一点嫌疑，还不能就认为是事实哩。

I am to pray you not to strain my speech
To grosser issues nor to larger reach
Than to suspicion.

OTHELLO I will not.

IAGO Should you do so, my lord,
My speech should fall into such vile success
As my thoughts aim not at.
Cassio's my worthy friend—
My lord, I see you're moved.

OTHELLO No, not much moved:
I do not think but Desdemona's honest.

IAGO Long live she so! and long live you to think so!

OTHELLO And yet, how nature erring from itself,—

IAGO Ay, there's the point: as—to be bold with you—
Not to affect many proposed matches
Of her own clime, complexion, and degree,
Whereto we see in all things nature tends—
Foh! one may smell in such a will most rank,
Foul disproportion thoughts unnatural.
But pardon me; I do not in position
Distinctly speak of her; though I may fear
Her will, recoiling to her better judgment,
May fall to match you with her country forms
And happily repent.

OTHELLO Farewell, farewell:
If more thou dost perceive, let me know more;
Set on thy wife to observe: leave me, Iago:

IAGO *[Going]* My lord, I take my leave.

OTHELLO Why did I marry? This honest creature doubtless
Sees and knows more, much more, than he unfolds.

IAGO *[Returning]*
My lord, I would I might entreat your honour

奥瑟罗 我不会的。

伊阿古 您要是这样，主帅，那么我的话就要引起不幸的后果，完全违反我的本意了。凯西奥是我的好朋友——主帅，我看您在动怒啦。

奥瑟罗 不，并不怎么动怒。我怎么也不能不相信苔丝狄蒙娜是贞洁的。

伊阿古 但愿她永远如此！但愿您永远这样想！

奥瑟罗 可是一个人往往容易迷失本性——

伊阿古 嗯，问题就在这儿。说句大胆的话，当初多少跟她同国族、同肤色、同阶级的人向她求婚，照我们看来，要是成功了，那真是天作之合，可是她都置之不理，这明明是违反常情的举动。嘿！从这儿就可以看到一个荒唐的意志、乖僻的习性和不近人情的思想。可是原谅我，我不一定指着她说；虽然我恐怕她因为一时的孟浪跟随了您，也许后来会觉得您在各方面不能符合她自己国中的标准而懊悔她的选择的错误。

奥瑟罗 再会，再会。要是你还观察到什么事，请让我知道；叫你的妻子留心察看。离开我，伊阿古。

伊阿古 主帅，我告辞了。（欲去）

奥瑟罗 我为什么要结婚呢？这个诚实的汉子所看到、所知道的事情，一定比他向我宣布出来的多得多。

伊阿古 （回转）主帅，我想请您最好把这件事情搁一搁，慢慢再说吧。凯西奥虽然应该让他复职，因为他对于这一个职位是非常胜

To scan this thing no further; leave it to time:
Though it be fit that Cassio have his place,
For sure, he fills it up with great ability,
Yet, if you please to hold him off awhile,
You shall by that perceive him and his means:
Note, if your lady strain his entertainment
With any strong or vehement importunity;
Much will be seen in that. In the mean time,
Let me be thought too busy in my fears—
As worthy cause I have to fear I am—
And hold her free, I do beseech your honour.

OTHELLO Fear not my government.

IAGO I once more take my leave.

Exit.

OTHELLO This fellow's of exceeding honesty,
And knows all qualities, with a learned spirit,
Of human dealings. If I do prove her haggard,
Though that her jesses were my dear heartstrings,
I'ld whistle her off and let her down the wind,
To pray at fortune. Haply, for I am black
And have not those soft parts of conversation
That chamberers have, or for I am declined
Into the vale of years,—yet that's not much—
She's gone. I am abused; and my relief
Must be to loathe her. O curse of marriage,
That we can call these delicate creatures ours,
And not their appetites! I had rather be a toad,
And live upon the vapour of a dungeon,
Than keep a corner in the thing I love
For others' uses. Yet, 'tis the plague of great ones;

任的。可是您要是愿意对他暂时延宕一下，就可以借此窥探他的真相，看他钻的是哪一条门路。您只要注意尊夫人在您面前是不是着力替他说情；从那上头就可以看出不少情事。现在请您只把我的意见认作无谓的过虑——我相信我的确太多疑了——仍旧把尊夫人看成一个清白无罪的人。

奥瑟罗 你放心吧，我不会失去自制的。

伊阿古 那么我告辞了。

下。

奥瑟罗 这是一个非常诚实的家伙，对于人情世故是再熟悉不过的了。要是我能够证明她是一头没有驯服的野鹰，虽然我用自己的心弦把她系住，我也要放她随风远去，追寻她自己的命运。也许因为我生得黑丑，缺少绅士们温柔风雅的谈吐；也许因为我年纪老了点儿——虽然还不算顶老——所以她才会背叛我；我已经自取其辱，只好割断对她这一段痴情。啊，结婚的烦恼！我们可以在名义上把这些可爱的人儿称为我们所有，却不能支配她们的爱憎喜恶！我宁愿做一只蛤蟆，呼吸牢室中的浊气，也不愿占住了自己心爱之物的一角，让别人把它享用。可是那是富贵者也不能幸免的灾祸，他们并不比贫贱者享有更多的特权；那是像死一样不可逃避的命运，我们一生下来就已经在冥冥中注定了要戴那顶倒霉的绿头巾。瞧！她来了。倘然她是不贞的，啊！那么上天在开自己的玩笑了。我不信。

Prerogativ'd are they less than the base;
'Tis destiny unshunnable, like death:
Even then this forked plague is fated to us
When we do quicken. Desdemona comes:
If she be false, O, then heaven mocks itself!
I'll not believe't.

Re-enter DESDEMONA and EMILIA.

DESDEMONA How now, my dear Othello!
Your dinner, and the generous islanders
By you invited, do attend your presence.

OTHELLO I am to blame.

DESDEMONA Why do you speak so faintly?
Are you not well?

OTHELLO I have a pain upon my forehead here.

DESDEMONA 'Faith, that's with watching; 'twill away again:
Let me but bind it hard, within this hour
It will be well.

OTHELLO Your napkin is too little:

He puts the handkerchief from him; and it drops.

Let it alone. Come, I'll go in with you.

DESDEMONA I am very sorry that you are not well.

Exeunt OTHELLO and DESDEMONA.

EMILIA I am glad I have found this napkin:
This was her first remembrance from the Moor:
My wayward husband hath a hundred times
Woo'd me to steal it; but she so loves the token,
For he conjured her she should ever keep it,
That she reserves it evermore about her

苔丝狄蒙娜及爱米利娅重上。

苔丝狄蒙娜 啊，我的亲爱的奥瑟罗！您所宴请的那些岛上的贵人们都在等着您去就席哩。

奥 瑟 罗 是我失礼了。

苔丝狄蒙娜 您怎么说话这样没有劲？您不大舒服吗？

奥 瑟 罗 我有点儿头痛。

苔丝狄蒙娜 那一定是因为睡少的缘故，不要紧的，让我替您绑紧了，一小时内就可以痊愈。

奥 瑟 罗 你的手帕太小了。

苔丝狄蒙娜手帕坠地。

随它去；来，我跟你一块儿进去。

苔丝狄蒙娜 您身子不舒服，我很懊恼。

奥瑟罗、苔丝狄蒙娜下。

爱米利娅 我很高兴我拾到了这方手帕，这是她从那摩尔人手里第一次得到的礼物。我那古怪的丈夫向我说过了不知多少好话，要我把它偷出来；可是她非常喜欢这玩意儿，因为他叫她永远保存好，所以她随时带在身边，一个人的时候就拿出来把它亲吻，对它说话。我要去把那花样描下来，再把它送给伊阿古；究竟他拿去有什么用，天才知道，我可不知道。我只不过为了讨他的喜欢。

To kiss and talk to. I'll have the work ta'en out,
And give't Iago: what he will do with it
Heaven knows, not I;
I nothing but to please his fantasy.

Re-enter Iago.

IAGO How now! what do you here alone?
EMILIA Do not you chide; I have a thing for you.
IAGO A thing for me? it is a common thing—
EMILIA Ha!
IAGO To have a foolish wife.
EMILIA O, is that all? What will you give me now
For the same handkerchief?
IAGO What handkerchief?
EMILIA What handkerchief?
Why, that the Moor first gave to Desdemona;
That which so often you did bid me steal.
IAGO Hast stol'n it from her?
EMILIA No, 'faith; she let it drop by negligence.
And, to the advantage, I, being here, took't up.
Look, here it is.
IAGO A good wench; give it me.
EMILIA What will you do with 't, that you have been so earnest
To have me filch it?
IAGO *[Snatching it]* Why, what's that to you?
EMILIA If it be not for some purpose of import,
Give't me again: poor lady, she'll run mad
When she shall lack it.
IAGO Be not acknown on 't; I have use for it.
Go, leave me.

Exit EMILIA.

伊阿古重上。

伊 阿 古 啊！你一个人在这儿干吗？

爱米利娅 不要骂，我有一件好东西给你。

伊 阿 古 一件好东西给我？一件不值钱的东西——

爱米利娅 嘿！

伊 阿 古 娶了一个愚蠢的老婆。

爱米利娅 啊！只落得这句话吗？要是我现在把那方手帕给了你，你给我什么东西？

伊 阿 古 什么手帕？

爱米利娅 什么手帕！就是那摩尔人第一次送给苔丝狄蒙娜，你老是叫我偷出来的那方手帕呀。

伊 阿 古 已经偷来了吗？

爱米利娅 不，不瞒你说，她自己不小心掉了下来，我正在旁边，乘此机会就把它拾起来了。瞧，这不是吗？

伊 阿 古 好妻子，给我。

爱米利娅 你一定要我偷了它来，究竟有什么用？

伊 阿 古 哼，那干你什么事？（夺帕）

爱米利娅 要是没有重要的用途，还是把它还了我吧。可怜的夫人！她失去这方手帕，准要发疯了。

伊 阿 古 不要说出来，我自有用处。去，离开我。

爱米利娅下。

I will in Cassio's lodging lose this napkin,
And let him find it. Trifles light as air
Are to the jealous confirmations strong
As proofs of holy writ: this may do something.
The Moor already changes with my poison:
Dangerous conceits are, in their natures, poisons.
Which at the first are scarce found to distaste,
But with a little act upon the blood.
Burn like the mines of Sulphur. I did say so:
Look, where he comes!

Re-enter OTHELLO.

Not poppy, nor mandragora,
Nor all the drowsy syrups of the world,
Shall ever medicine thee to that sweet sleep
Which thou ow'dst yesterday.

OTHELLO Ha! ha! false to me?

IAGO Why, how now, general! no more of that.

OTHELLO Avaunt! be gone! thou hast set me on the rack:
I swear 'tis better to be much abused
Than but to know't a little.

IAGO How now, my lord!

OTHELLO What sense had I of her stol'n hours of lust?
I saw't not, thought it not, it harm'd not me:
I slept the next night well, was free and merry;
I found not Cassio's kisses on her lips:
He that is robb'd, not wanting what is stol'n,
Let him not know't, and he's not robb'd at all.

IAGO I am sorry to hear this.

OTHELLO I had been happy, if the general camp,
Pioners and all, had tasted her sweet body,

我要把这手帕丢在凯西奥的寓所里，让他找到它。像空气一样轻的小事，对于一个嫉妒的人，也会变成天书一样坚强的确证；也许这就可以引起一场是非。这摩尔人已经中了我的毒药的毒，他的心理上已经发生变化了；危险的思想本来就是一种毒药，虽然在开始的时候尝不到什么苦涩的味道，可是渐渐地在血液里活动起来，就会像硫矿一样轰然爆发。我的话果然不差，瞧，他又来了！

奥瑟罗重上。

罂粟、曼陀罗或是世上一切使人昏迷的药草，都不能使你得到昨天晚上你还安然享受的酣眠。

奥瑟罗 嘿！嘿！对我不贞？

伊阿古 啊，怎么，主帅！别老想着那件事啦。

奥瑟罗 去！滚开！你害得我好苦。与其知道得不明不白，还是糊里糊涂受人家欺弄的好。

伊阿古 怎么，主帅！

奥瑟罗 她瞒着我跟人家私通，我不是一无知觉吗？我没有看见，没有想到，它对我漠不相干。到了晚上，我还是睡得好好的，逍遥自得，无忧无虑，在她的嘴唇上找不到凯西奥吻过的痕迹。被盗的人要是不知道偷儿盗去了他什么东西，旁人也不去让他知道，他就等于没有被盗一样。

伊阿古 我很抱歉听见您说这样的话。

奥瑟罗 要是全营的将士，从最低微的工兵起，都曾领略过她的肉体的美趣，只要我一无所知，我还是快乐的。啊！从今以后，永别了，

So I had nothing known. O, now, for ever
Farewell the tranquil mind! farewell content!
Farewell the plumed troop, and the big wars,
That make ambition virtue! O, farewell!
Farewell the neighing steed, and the shrill trump,
The spirit-stirring drum, the ear-piercing fife,
The royal banner, and all quality,
Pride, pomp and circumstance of glorious war!
And, O you mortal engines, whose rude throats
The immortal Jove's dead clamours counterfeit,
Farewell! Othello's occupation's gone!

IAGO Is't possible, my lord?

OTHELLO Villain, be sure thou prove my love a whore,
Be sure of it; give me the ocular proof:
Or by the worth of man's eternal soul,
Thou hadst been better have been born a dog
Than answer my waked wrath!

IAGO Is't come to this?

OTHELLO Make me to see't; or, at the least, so prove it,
That the probation bear no hinge nor loop
To hang a doubt on; or woe upon thy life!

IAGO My noble lord,—

OTHELLO If thou dost slander her and torture me,
Never pray more; abandon all remorse;
On horror's head horrors accumulate;
Do deeds to make heaven weep, all earth amazed;
For nothing canst thou to damnation add
Greater than that.

IAGO O grace! O heaven forgive me!
Are you a man? have you a soul or sense?
God be wi' you; take mine office. O wretched fool.
That liv'st to make thine honesty a vice!

宁静的心绪！永别了，平和的幸福！永别了，威武的大军、激发壮志的战争！啊，永别了！永别了，长嘶的骏马、锐厉的号角、惊魂的鼙鼓、刺耳的横笛、庄严的大旗和一切战阵上的威仪！还有你，杀人的巨炮啊，你的残暴的喉管里摹仿着天神乔武的怒吼，永别了！奥瑟罗的事业已经完了。

伊阿古 难道一至于此吗，主帅？

奥瑟罗 恶人，你必须证明我的爱人是一个淫妇，你必须给我目击的证据。否则凭着人类永生的灵魂起誓，我的激起了的怒火将要喷射在你的身上，使你悔恨自己当初不曾投胎做一条狗！

伊阿古 竟会到了这样的地步吗？

奥瑟罗 让我亲眼看见这种事实，或者至少给我无可置疑的切实的证据，不这样可不行；否则我要活活要你的命！

伊阿古 尊贵的主帅——

奥瑟罗 你要是故意捏造谣言，毁坏她的名誉，使我受到难堪的痛苦，那么你再不要祈祷吧。放弃一切恻隐之心，让各种骇人听闻的罪恶丛集于你罪恶的一身，尽管做一些使上天悲泣、使人世惊愕的暴行吧，因为你现在已经罪大恶极，没有什么可以使你在地狱里沉沦得更深的了。

伊阿古 天啊！您是一个汉子吗？您有灵魂吗？您有知觉吗？上帝和您同在！我也不要做这劳什子的旗官了。啊，倒霉的傻瓜！你一生只想做个老实人，人家却把你的老实当作了罪恶！啊，丑恶的世界！注意，注意，世人啊！说老实话，做老实人，是一件危险

O monstrous world! Take note, take note, O world,
To be direct and honest is not safe.
I thank you for this profit; and from hence
I'll love no friend, sith love breeds such offence.

OTHELLO Nay, stay: thou shouldst be honest.

IAGO I should be wise, for honesty's a fool
And loses that it works for.

OTHELLO By the world,
I think my wife be honest and think she is not;
I think that thou art just and think thou art not.
I'll have some proof. Her name, that was as fresh
As Dian's visage, is now begrimed and black
As mine own face. If there be cords, or knives,
Poison, or fire, or suffocating streams,
I'll not endure it. Would I were satisfied!

IAGO I see, sir, you are eaten up with passion:
I do repent me that I put it to you.
You would be satisfied?

OTHELLO Would! nay, I will.

IAGO And may: but, how? how satisfied, my lord?
Would you, the supervisor, grossly gape on—
Behold her topp'd?

OTHELLO Death and damnation! O!

IAGO It were a tedious difficulty, I think,
To bring them to that prospect: damn them then,
If ever mortal eyes do see them bolster
More than their own! What then? how then?
What shall I say? Where's satisfaction?
It is impossible you should see this,
Were they as prime as goats, as hot as monkeys,
As salt as wolves in pride, and fools as gross
As ignorance made drunk. But yet, I say,

的事哩。谢谢您给我这一个有益的教训，既然善意反而遭人嗔怪，从此以后，我再也不对什么朋友掬献我的真情了。

奥瑟罗 不，且慢，你应该做一个老实人。

伊阿古 我应该做一个聪明人，因为老实人就是傻瓜，虽然一片好心，结果还是自己吃了亏。

奥瑟罗 我想我的妻子是贞洁的，可是又疑心她不大贞洁；我想你是诚实的，可是又疑心你不大诚实。我一定要得到一些证据。她的名誉本来是像狄安娜的容颜一样皎洁的，现在已经染上污垢，像我自己的脸一样黝黑了。要是这儿有绳子、刀子、毒药、火焰或是使人窒息的河水，我一定不能忍受下去。但愿我能够扫空这一块疑团！

伊阿古 主帅，我看您完全被感情所支配了。我很后悔不该惹起您的疑心。那么您愿意知道究竟吗？

奥瑟罗 愿意！嘿，我一定要知道。

伊阿古 那倒是可以的。可是怎样办呢？怎样才算知道了呢，主帅？您还是眼睁睁地当场看她被人奸污吗？

奥瑟罗 啊！该死该死！

伊阿古 叫他们当场出丑，我想很不容易；他们干这种事，总是要避人眼目的。那么怎么样呢？又怎么办呢？我应该怎么说呢？怎样才可以拿到真凭实据？即使他们像山羊一样风骚，猴子一样好色，豺狼一样贪淫，即使他们是糊涂透顶的傻瓜，您也看不到他们这一幕把戏。可是我说，有了确凿的线索，就可以探出事实的真相；要是这一类间接的旁证可以替您解除疑惑，那倒是不难让你得到的。

If imputation and strong circumstances,
Which lead directly to the door of truth,
Will give you satisfaction, you may have't.

OTHELLO Give me a living reason she's disloyal.

IAGO I do not like the office:
But, sith I am enter'd in this cause so far,
Prick'd to't by foolish honesty and love,
I will go on. I lay with Cassio lately;
And, being troubled with a raging tooth,
I could not sleep.
There are a kind of men so loose of soul,
That in their sleeps will mutter their affairs:
One of this kind is Cassio:
In sleep I heard him say 'Sweet Desdemona,
Let us be wary, let us hide our loves;'
And then, sir, would he gripe and wring my hand,
Cry 'O sweet creature!' and then kiss me hard,
As if he pluck'd up kisses by the roots,
That grew upon my lips: then laid his leg
Over my thigh, and sigh'd, and kiss'd; and then
Cried 'Cursed fate that gave thee to the Moor!'

OTHELLO O monstrous! monstrous!

IAGO Nay, this was but his dream.

OTHELLO But this denoted a foregone conclusion:
'Tis a shrewd doubt, though it be but a dream.

IAGO And this may help to thicken other proofs
That do demonstrate thinly.

OTHELLO I'll tear her all to pieces.

IAGO Nay, but be wise: yet we see nothing done;
She may be honest yet. Tell me but this,
Have you not sometimes seen a handkerchief

奥瑟罗 给我一个充分的理由，证明她已经失节。

伊阿古 我不欢喜这件差使。可是既然愚蠢的忠心已经把我拉进了这一桩纠纷里去，我也不能再保持沉默了。最近我曾经和凯西奥同过榻。我因为牙痛不能入睡；世上有一种人，他们的灵魂是不能保守秘密的，往往会在睡梦之中吐露他们的私事，凯西奥也就是这一种人。我听见他在梦寐中说，“亲爱的苔丝狄蒙娜，我们须要小心，不要让别人窥破了我们的爱情！”于是，主帅，他就紧紧地捏住我的手，嘴里喊，“啊，可爱的人儿！”然后狠狠地吻着我，好像那些吻是长在我的嘴唇上，他恨不得把它们连根拔起一样；然后他又把他的脚搁在我的大腿上，叹一口气，亲一个吻，喊一声“该死的命运，把你给了那摩尔人！”

奥瑟罗 啊，可恶！可恶！

伊阿古 不，这不过是他的梦。

奥瑟罗 但是过去发生过什么事就可想而知；虽然只是一个梦，怎么能不叫人起疑呢。

伊阿古 本来只是很无谓的事，现在这样一看，也就大有文章了。

奥瑟罗 我要把她碎尸万段。

伊阿古 不，您不能太鲁莽了。我们还没有看见实际的行动，也许她还是贞洁的。告诉我这一点：您有没有看见过在尊夫人的手里有一方绣着草莓花样的手帕？

Spotted with strawberries in your wife's hand?

OTHELLO I gave her such a one; 'twas my first gift.

IAGO I know not that; but such a handkerchief—
I am sure it was your wife's—did I today
See Cassio wipe his beard with.

OTHELLO If it be that—

IAGO If it be that, or any that was hers,
It speaks against her with the other proofs.

OTHELLO O, that the slave had forty thousand lives!
One is too poor, too weak for my revenge.
Now do I see 'tis true. Look here, Iago;
All my fond love thus do I blow to heaven.
'Tis gone.
Arise, black vengeance, from thy hollow cell!
Yield up, O love, thy crown and hearted throne
To tyrannous hate! Swell, bosom, with thy fraught,
For 'tis of aspics' tongues!

IAGO Yet be content.

OTHELLO O, blood, blood, blood!

IAGO Patience, I say; your mind perhaps may change.

OTHELLO Never, Iago: Like to the Pontic sea,
Whose icy current and compulsive course
Ne'er feels retiring ebb, but keeps due on
To the Propontic and the Hellespont,
Even so my bloody thoughts, with violent pace,
Shall ne'er look back, ne'er ebb to humble love,
Till that a capable and wide revenge
Swallow them up. Now, by yond marble heaven,
[Kneels] In the due reverence of a sacred vow
I here engage my words.

IAGO Do not rise yet.
[Kneels] Witness, you ever-burning lights above,

奥瑟罗 我给过她这样一方手帕，那是我第一次送给她的礼物。

伊阿古 那我不知道，可是今天我看见凯西奥用这样一方手帕抹他的胡子，我相信它一定就是尊夫人的。

奥瑟罗 假如就是那一方手帕——

伊阿古 假如就是那一方手帕，或者是其他她所用过的手帕，那么又是一个对她不利的证据了。

奥瑟罗 啊，我但愿那家伙有四万条生命！单单让他死一次是发泄不了我的愤怒的。现在我明白这件事情全然是真的了。瞧，伊阿古，我把我的全部痴情向天空中吹散；它已经随风消失了。黑暗的复仇，从你的幽窟之中升起来吧！爱情啊，把你的王冠和你的心灵深处的宝座让给残暴的憎恨吧！胀起来吧，我的胸膛，因为你已经满载着毒蛇的螫舌！

伊阿古 请不要生气。

奥瑟罗 啊，血！血！血！

伊阿古 忍耐点儿吧，也许您的意见会改变过来的。

奥瑟罗 决不，伊阿古。正像黑海的寒涛滚滚奔流，奔进马尔马拉海，直冲达达尼尔海峡，永远不会后退一样，我的风驰电掣的流血的思想，在复仇的目的没有充分达到以前，也决不会踟蹰回顾，化为绕指的柔情。（跪）苍天在上，我倘不能报复这奇耻大辱，誓不偷生人世。

伊阿古 且慢起来。（跪）亘古炳耀的日月星辰，环抱宇宙的风云雨雾，请你们为我作证：从现在起，伊阿古愿意尽心竭力，为被欺的奥

You elements that clip us round about,
Witness that here Iago doth give up
The execution of his wit, hands, heart,
To wrong'd Othello's service! Let him command,
And to obey shall be in me remorse,
What bloody business ever.

They rise.

OTHELLO I greet thy love,
Not with vain thanks, but with acceptance bounteous,
And will upon the instant put thee to't:
Within these three days let me hear thee say
That Cassio's not alive.

IAGO My friend is dead; 'tis done at your request:
But let her live.

OTHELLO Damn her, lewd minx! O, damn her!
Come, go with me apart; I will withdraw,
To furnish me with some swift means of death
For the fair devil. Now art thou my lieutenant.

IAGO I am your own for ever.

Exeunt.

瑟罗效劳；无论他叫我做什么残酷的事，我一切唯命是从。

众人起身。

奥瑟罗 我不用空口的感谢接受你的好意，为了表示我的诚心的嘉纳，我要请你立刻履行你的诺言：在这三天以内，让我听见你说凯西奥已经不在人世。

伊阿古 我的朋友的死已经决定了，因为这是您的意旨。可是放她活命吧。

奥瑟罗 该死的淫妇！啊，咒死她！来，跟我去，我要为这美貌的魔鬼想出一个干脆的死法。现在你是我的副将了。

伊阿古 我永远是您的忠仆。

同下。

SCENE IV

Before the castle.
Enter DESDEMONA, EMILIA, and Clown.

DESDEMONA Do you know, sirrah, where Lieutenant Cassio lies?

Clown I dare not say he lies any where.

DESDEMONA Why, man?

Clown He's a soldier, and for one to say a soldier lies, is stabbing.

DESDEMONA Go to: where lodges he?

Clown To tell you where he lodges, is to tell you where I lie.

DESDEMONA Can any thing be made of this?

Clown I know not where he lodges, and for me to devise a lodging and say he lies here or he lies there, were to lie in mine own throat.

DESDEMONA Can you inquire him out, and be edified by report?

Clown I will catechise the world for him; that is, make questions, and by them answer.

DESDEMONA Seek him, bid him come hither: tell him I have moved my lord on his behalf, and hope all will be well.

Clown To do this is within the compass of man's wit: and therefore I will attempt the doing it.

Exit.

DESDEMONA Where should I lose that handkerchief, Emilia?

EMILIA I know not, madam.

DESDEMONA Believe me, I had rather have lost my purse
Full of cruzadoes: and, but my noble Moor
Is true of mind and made of no such baseness
As jealous creatures are, it were enough
To put him to ill thinking.

第四场

城堡前。

苔丝狄蒙娜、爱米利娅及小丑上。

苔丝狄蒙娜 喂，你知道凯西奥副将的家在什么地方吗？

小　丑 我可不敢说他有“家”。

苔丝狄蒙娜 为什么，好人儿？

小　丑 他是个军人，要是说军人心中有“假”，那可是性命出入的事儿。

苔丝狄蒙娜 好吧，那么他住在什么地方呢？

小　丑 告诉您他住在什么地方，就是告诉您我在撒谎。

苔丝狄蒙娜 那是什么意思？

小　丑 我不知道他住在什么地方。要是胡乱想出一个地方来，说他“家”住在这儿，“家”住在那儿，那就是我存心说“假”话了。

苔丝狄蒙娜 你可以打听打听他在什么地方呀。

小　丑 好，我就去到处向人家打听——那是说，去盘问人家，看他们怎么回答我。

苔丝狄蒙娜 找到了他，你就叫他到这儿来，对他说我已经替他在将军面前说过情了，大概可以得到圆满的结果。

小　丑 干这件事是一个人的智力所能及的，所以我愿意去干一下。

下。

苔丝狄蒙娜 我究竟在什么地方掉了那方手帕呢，爱米利娅？

爱米利娅 我不知道，夫人。

苔丝狄蒙娜 相信我，我宁愿失去我的一满袋金币。倘然我的摩尔人不是这样一个光明磊落的汉子，倘然他也像那些多疑善妒的卑鄙男人一样，这是很可以引起他的疑心的。

EMILIA Is he not jealous?

DESDEMONA Who, he? I think the sun where he was born
Drew all such humours from him.

EMILIA Look, where he comes.

DESDEMONA I will not leave him now till Cassio
Be call'd to him.

Enter OTHELLO.

DESDEMONA How is't with you, my lord

OTHELLO Well, my good lady.
[Aside] O, hardness to dissemble!—
How do you, Desdemona?

DESDEMONA Well, my good lord.

OTHELLO Give me your hand: this hand is moist, my lady.

DESDEMONA It yet hath felt no age nor known no sorrow.

OTHELLO This argues fruitfulness and liberal heart:
Hot, hot, and moist: this hand of yours requires
A sequester from liberty, fasting and prayer,
Much castigation, exercise devout;
For here's a young and sweating devil here,
That commonly rebels. 'Tis a good hand,
A frank one.

DESDEMONA You may, indeed, say so;
For 'twas that hand that gave away my heart.

OTHELLO A liberal hand: the hearts of old gave hands;
But our new heraldry is hands, not hearts.

DESDEMONA I cannot speak of this. Come now, your promise.

OTHELLO What promise, chuck?

DESDEMONA I have sent to bid Cassio come speak with you.

OTHELLO I have a salt and sorry rheum offends me;
Lend me thy handkerchief.

爱米利娅 他不会嫉妒吗？

苔丝狄蒙娜 谁！他？我想在他生长的地方，那灼热的阳光已经把这种气质完全从他身上吸去了。

爱米利娅 瞧！他来了。

苔丝狄蒙娜 我在他没有把凯西奥叫到他跟前来以前，决不离开他一步。

奥瑟罗上。

苔丝狄蒙娜 您好吗，我的主？

奥瑟罗 好，我的好夫人。（旁白）啊，装假脸真不容易！——你好，苔丝狄蒙娜？

苔丝狄蒙娜 我好，我的好夫君。

奥瑟罗 把你的手给我。这手很潮润呢，我的夫人。

苔丝狄蒙娜 它还没有感到老年的侵袭，也没有受过忧伤的损害。

奥瑟罗 这一只手表明它的主人是胸襟宽大而心肠慷慨的；这么热，这么潮。奉劝夫人努力克制邪心，常常斋戒祷告，反躬自责，礼拜神明，因为这儿有一个年少风流的魔鬼，惯会在人们血液里捣乱。这是一只好手，一只很慷慨的手。

苔丝狄蒙娜 您真的可以这样说，因为就是这一只手把我的心献给您的。

奥瑟罗 一只慷慨的手。从前的姑娘把手给人，同时把心也一起给了他。现在时世变了，得到一位姑娘的手的，不一定能够得到她的心。

苔丝狄蒙娜 这种话我不会说。来，您答应我的事怎么样啦？

奥瑟罗 我答应你什么，乖乖？

苔丝狄蒙娜 我已经叫人去请凯西奥来跟您谈谈了。

奥瑟罗 我的眼睛有些胀痛，老是淌着眼泪。把你的手帕借给我一用。

DESDEMONA Here, my lord.

OTHELLO That which I gave you.

DESDEMONA I have it not about me.

OTHELLO Not?

DESDEMONA No, indeed, my lord.

OTHELLO That is a fault.
That handkerchief
Did an Egyptian to my mother give;
She was a charmer, and could almost read
The thoughts of people: she told her, while
she kept it,
'Twould make her amiable and subdue my father
Entirely to her love, but if she lost it
Or made gift of it, my father's eye
Should hold her loathed and his spirits should hunt
After new fancies: she, dying, gave it me;
And bid me, when my fate would have me wive,
To give it her. I did so: and take heed on't;
Make it a darling like your precious eye;
To lose't or give't away were such perdition
As nothing else could match.

DESDEMONA Is't possible?

OTHELLO 'Tis true: there's magic in the web of it:
A sibyl, that had number'd in the world
The sun to course two hundred compasses,
In her prophetic fury sew'd the work;
The worms were hallow'd that did breed the silk;
And it was dyed in mummy which the skilful
Conserved of maidens' hearts.

DESDEMONA Indeed! is't true?

OTHELLO Most veritable; therefore look to't well.

DESDEMONA Then would to God that I had never seen't!

苔丝狄蒙娜　这儿，我的主。

奥 瑟 罗　我给你的那一方呢？

苔丝狄蒙娜　我没有带在身边。

奥 瑟 罗　没有带？

苔丝狄蒙娜　真的没有带，我的主。

奥 瑟 罗　那你可错了。那方手帕是一个埃及女人送给我的母亲的；她是一个能够洞察人心的女巫，她对我的母亲说，当她保存着这方手帕的时候，它可以使她得到我的父亲的欢心，享受专房的爱宠，可是她要是失去了它，或是把它送给旁人，我的父亲就要对她发生憎厌，他的心就要另觅新欢了。她在临死的时候把它传给我，叫我有了妻子以后，就把它交给新妇。我遵照她的吩咐给了你，所以你必须格外小心，珍惜它像珍惜你自己宝贵的眼睛一样；万一失去了，或是送给别人，那就难免遭到一场无比的灾祸。

苔丝狄蒙娜　真会有这种事吗？

奥 瑟 罗　真的，这一方小小的手帕，却有神奇的魔力织在里面。它是一个二百岁的神巫在一阵心血来潮的时候缝就的；它那一缕缕的丝线，也不是世间的凡蚕所吐；织成以后，它曾经在用处女的心炼成的丹液里浸过。

苔丝狄蒙娜　当真！这是真的吗？

奥 瑟 罗　绝对的真实！所以留心藏好它吧。

苔丝狄蒙娜　上帝啊，但愿我从来没有见过它！

OTHELLO Ha! wherefore?

DESDEMONA Why do you speak so startingly and rash?

OTHELLO Is't lost? is't gone? speak, is it out o' the way?

DESDEMONA Heaven bless us!

OTHELLO Say you?

DESDEMONA It is not lost; but what an if it were?

OTHELLO How!

DESDEMONA I say, it is not lost.

OTHELLO Fetch't, let me see't.

DESDEMONA Why, so I can, sir, but I will not now.
This is a trick to put me from my suit:
Pray you, let Cassio be received again.

OTHELLO Fetch me the handkerchief: my mind misgives.

DESDEMONA Come, come;
You'll never meet a more sufficient man.

OTHELLO The handkerchief!

DESDEMONA I pray, talk me of Cassio.

OTHELLO The handkerchief!

DESDEMONA A man that all his time
Hath founded his good fortunes on your love,
Shared dangers with you,—

OTHELLO The handkerchief!

DESDEMONA In sooth, you are to blame.

OTHELLO Away!

Exit.

EMILIA Is not this man jealous?

DESDEMONA I ne'er saw this before.
Sure, there's some wonder in this handkerchief:
I am most unhappy in the loss of it.

EMILIA 'Tis not a year or two shows us a man:

奥瑟罗　嘿！为什么？

苔丝狄蒙娜　您为什么说得这样暴躁？

奥瑟罗　它已经失去了吗？不见了吗？说，它是不是已经丢了？

苔丝狄蒙娜　上天祝福我们！

奥瑟罗　你说。

苔丝狄蒙娜　它没有失去，可是要是失去了，那可怎么办呢？

奥瑟罗　怎么！

苔丝狄蒙娜　我说它没有失去。

奥瑟罗　去把它拿来给我看。

苔丝狄蒙娜　我可以去把它拿来，可是现在我不高兴。这是一个诡计，要想把我的要求赖了过去。请您把凯西奥重新录用了吧。

奥瑟罗　给我把那手帕拿来。我在起疑心了。

苔丝狄蒙娜　得啦，得啦，您再也找不到一个比他更能干的人。

奥瑟罗　手帕！

苔丝狄蒙娜　请您还是跟我谈谈凯西奥的事情吧。

奥瑟罗　手帕！

苔丝狄蒙娜　他一向把自己的前途寄托在您的眷爱上，又跟着您同甘共苦，历尽艰辛——

奥瑟罗　手帕！

苔丝狄蒙娜　凭良心说，您也太不该。

奥瑟罗　去！

下。

爱米利娅　这个人在嫉妒吗？

苔丝狄蒙娜　我从来没有见过他这样子。这手帕一定有些不可思议的魔力，我真倒霉把它丢了。

爱米利娅　好的男人一两年里头也难得碰见一个。男人是一张胃，我们是

They are all but stomachs, and we all but food;
To eat us hungerly, and when they are full,
They belch us. Look you, Cassio and my husband!

Enter CASSIO and IAGO.

IAGO There is no other way; 'tis she must do't:
And, lo, the happiness! go, and importune her.

DESDEMONA How now, good Cassio! what's the news with you?

CASSIO Madam, my former suit: I do beseech you
That by your virtuous means I may again
Exist, and be a member of his love
Whom I with all the office of my heart
Entirely honour: I would not be delay'd.
If my offence be of such mortal kind
That nor my service past, nor present sorrows,
Nor purposed merit in futurity,
Can ransom me into his love again,
But to know so must be my benefit;
So shall I clothe me in a forced content,
And shut myself up in some other course,
To fortune's alms.

DESDEMONA Alas, thrice-gentle Cassio!
My advocation is not now in tune;
My lord is not my lord; nor should I know him,
Were he in favour as in humour alter'd.
So help me every spirit sanctified,
As I have spoken for you all my best
And stood within the blank of his displeasure
For my free speech! you must awhile be patient:
What I can do I will; and more I will
Than for myself I dare: let that suffice you.

一块肉；他们贪馋地把我们吞下去，吃饱了，就把我们呕出来。您瞧！凯西奥跟我的丈夫来啦。

伊阿古及凯西奥上。

伊阿古　没有别的法子，只好央求她出力。瞧！好运气！去求求她吧。

苔丝狄蒙娜　啊，好凯西奥！您有什么见教？

凯西奥　夫人，我还是要向您重提我的原来的请求，希望您发挥鼎力，让我重新做人，能够在我所尊敬的主帅麾下再邀恩眷。我不能这样延宕下去了。假如我果然罪大恶极，无论过去的微劳、现在的悔恨或是将来立功自赎的决心，都不能博取他的矜怜宽谅，那么我也希望得到一个明白的答复，我就死心塌地向别处去乞讨命运的布施了。

苔丝狄蒙娜　唉，善良的凯西奥！我的话已经变成刺耳的烦渎了；我的丈夫已经不是我的丈夫，要是他的面貌也像他的脾气一样变了样，我简直要不认识他了。愿神灵保佑我！我已经尽力替您说话；为了我的言辞的戆拙，我已经遭到他的憎恶。您必须暂时忍耐；只要是我力量所及的事，我都愿意为您一试；请您相信我，倘然那是我自己的事情，我也不会这样热心的。这样，您心里也该满意了吧。

IAGO Is my lord angry?

EMILIA He went hence but now,
And certainly in strange unquietness.

IAGO Can he be angry? I have seen the cannon,
When it hath blown his ranks into the air,
And, like the devil, from his very arm
Puff'd his own brother:—and can he be angry?
Something of moment then: I will go meet him:
There's matter in't indeed, if he be angry.

DESDEMONA I prithee, do so.
[Exit IAGO] Something, sure, of state,
Either from Venice, or some unhatch'd practise
Made demonstrable here in Cyprus to him,
Hath puddled his clear spirit: and in such cases
Men's natures wrangle with inferior things,
Though great ones are their object. 'Tis even so;
For let our finger ache, and it indues
Our other healthful members even to that sense
Of pain: nay, we must think men are not gods,
Nor of them look for such observances
As fit the bridal. Beshrew me much, Emilia,
I was, unhandsome warrior as I am,
Arraigning his unkindness with my soul;
But now I find I had suborn'd the witness,
And he's indicted falsely.

EMILIA Pray heaven it be state-matters, as you think,
And no conception nor no jealous toy Concerning you.

DESDEMONA Alas the day! I never gave him cause.

EMILIA But jealous souls will not be answer'd so;
They are not ever jealous for the cause,
But jealous for they are jealous: 'tis a monster
Begot upon itself, born on itself.

伊阿古 主帅发怒了吗？

爱米利娅 他刚才从这儿走开，他的神气暴躁异常。

伊阿古 他会发怒吗？我曾经看见大炮冲散他的队伍，像魔鬼一样把他的兄弟从他身边轰掉，他仍旧不动声色。他也会发怒吗？那么一定出了什么重大的事情了。我要去看看他。他要是发怒，一定有些缘故。

苔丝狄蒙娜 请你就去吧。（伊阿古下）一定是威尼斯有什么国家大事，或是他在这儿塞浦路斯发现了什么秘密的阴谋，扰乱了他的清明的神志。人们在这种情形之下，往往会为了一些小事而生气，虽然实际激怒他们的却是其他更大的原因。正是这样，我们一个指头疼痛的时候，全身都会觉得难受。我们不能把男人当作完善的天神，也不能希望他们永远像新婚之夜那样殷勤体贴。爱米利娅，我真该死，我可真是个不体面的“战士”，会在心里抱怨他的无情；现在我才觉悟我是收买了假见证，让他受了冤枉。

爱米利娅 谢天谢地，但愿果然像您所想的，是为了些国家的事情，不是因为对您起了疑心。

苔丝狄蒙娜 唉！我从来没有给过他一些可以使他怀疑的理由。

爱米利娅 是多疑的人是不会因此而满足的！他们往往不是因为有了什么理由而嫉妒，只是为了嫉妒而嫉妒，那是一个凭空而来、自生自长的怪物。

DESDEMONA Heaven keep that monster from Othello's mind!

EMILIA Lady, amen.

DESDEMONA I will go seek him. Cassio, walk hereabout:
If I do find him fit, I'll move your suit
And seek to effect it to my uttermost.

CASSIO I humbly thank your ladyship.

Exeunt DESDEMONA and EMILIA.
Enter BIANCA.

BIANCA Save you, friend Cassio!

CASSIO What make you from home?
How is it with you, my most fair Bianca?
I' faith, sweet love, I was coming to your house.

BIANCA And I was going to your lodging, Cassio.
What, keep a week away? seven days and nights?
Eight score eight hours? and lovers' absent hours,
More tedious than the dial eight score times?
O weary reckoning!

CASSIO Pardon me, Bianca:
I have this while with leaden thoughts been press'd:
But I shall, in a more continuate time,
Strike off this score of absence. Sweet Bianca,
Giving her DESDEMONA's handkerchief
Take me this work out.

BIANCA O Cassio, whence came this?
This is some token from a newer friend:
To the felt absence now I feel a cause:
Is't come to this? Well, well.

CASSIO Go to, woman!
Throw your vile guesses in the devil's teeth,
From whence you have them. You are jealous now
That this is from some mistress, some remembrance:

苔丝狄蒙娜 愿上天保佑奥瑟罗，不要让这怪物钻进他的心里！

爱米利娅 阿门，夫人。

苔丝狄蒙娜 我去找他去。凯西奥，您在这儿走走；要是我看见自己可以跟他说几句话，我会向他提起您的请求，尽力给您转圜就是了。

凯 西 奥 多谢夫人。

苔丝狄蒙娜、爱米利娅下。
比恩卡上。

比恩卡 你好，凯西奥朋友！

凯 西 奥 你怎么不在家里？你好，我的最娇美的比恩卡？不骗你，亲爱的，我正要到你家里来呢。

比恩卡 我也是要到你的尊寓去的，凯西奥。什么！一个星期不来看我？七天七夜？一百六十八个小时？在相思里挨过的时辰，比时钟是要慢上一百六十倍的。啊，这一笔算不清的糊涂账！

凯 西 奥 对不起，比恩卡，这几天来我实在心事太重，改日加倍补报你就是了。亲爱的比恩卡，（以苔丝狄蒙娜手帕授比恩卡）替我把这手帕上的花样描下来。

比恩卡 啊，凯西奥！这是什么地方来的？这一定是哪个新相好送给你的礼物；我现在明白你不来看我的缘故了。有这等事吗？好，好。

凯 西 奥 得啦，女人！把你这种瞎疑心丢还给魔鬼吧。你在吃醋了，你以为这是什么情人送给我的纪念品，不，凭着我的良心发誓，比恩卡。

No, in good troth, Bianca.

BIANCA Why, whose is it?

CASSIO I know not, sweet: I found it in my chamber.
I like the work well: ere it be demanded—
As like enough it will—I'ld have it copied:
Take it, and do't; and leave me for this time.

BIANCA Leave you! wherefore?

CASSIO I do attend here on the general;
And think it no addition, nor my wish,
To have him see me woman'd.

BIANCA Why, I pray you?

CASSIO Not that I love you not.

BIANCA But that you do not love me.
I pray you, bring me on the way a little,
And say if I shall see you soon at night.

CASSIO 'Tis but a little way that I can bring you;
For I attend here: but I'll see you soon.

BIANCA 'Tis very good; I must be circumstanced.

Exeunt.

比恩卡 那么这是谁的？

凯 西 奥 我不知道，亲爱的；我在寝室里找到它。那花样我很喜欢，我想乘失主没有来问我讨还以前，把它描了下来。请你拿去给我描一描。现在请你暂时离开我。

比恩卡 离开你！为什么？

凯 西 奥 我在这儿等候主帅到来，让他看见我有女人陪着，恐怕不大方便，我不愿意这样。

比恩卡 为什么？我倒要请问。

凯 西 奥 不是因为我不爱你。

比恩卡 只是因为你并不爱我。请你陪我稍为走一段路，告诉我今天晚上你来不来看我。

凯 西 奥 我只能陪你稍走几步，因为我在这儿等人，可是我就会来看你的。

比恩卡 那很好，我也不能勉强你。

各下。

ACT Ⅳ　第四幕

SCENE I

Cyprus. Before the castle.
Enter OTHELLO and IAGO.

IAGO Will you think so?
OTHELLO Think so, Iago!
IAGO What,
To kiss in private?
OTHELLO An unauthorized kiss.
IAGO Or to be naked with her friend in bed
An hour or more, not meaning any harm?
OTHELLO Naked in bed, Iago, and not mean harm!
It is hypocrisy against the devil:
They that mean virtuously, and yet do so,
The devil their virtue tempts, and they tempt heaven.
IAGO So they do nothing, 'tis a venial slip:
But if I give my wife a handkerchief,—
OTHELLO What then?
IAGO Why, then, 'tis hers, my lord; and, being hers,
She may, I think, bestow't on any man.
OTHELLO She is protectress of her honour too:
May she give that?
IAGO Her honour is an essence that's not seen;
They have it very oft that have it not:
But, for the handkerchief,—
OTHELLO By heaven, I would most gladly have forgot it.
Thou said'st, it comes o'er my memory,
As doth the raven o'er the infected house,
Boding to all—he had my handkerchief.
IAGO Ay, what of that?
OTHELLO That's not so good now.

第一场

塞浦路斯。城堡前。

奥瑟罗及伊阿古上。

伊阿古 您愿意这样想吗？

奥瑟罗 这样想，伊阿古！

伊阿古 什么！背着人接吻？

奥瑟罗 这样的接吻是为礼法所不许的。

伊阿古 脱光了衣服，和她的朋友睡在一床，经过一个多小时，却一点不起邪念？

奥瑟罗 伊阿古，脱光衣服睡在床上，还会不起邪念！这明明是对魔鬼的假意矜持；他们的本心是规矩的，可偏是做出了这种勾当；魔鬼欺骗了这两个规规矩矩的人，而他们就去欺骗上天。

伊阿古 要是他们不及于乱，那还不过是一个小小的过失。可是假如我把一方手帕给了我的妻子——

奥瑟罗 给了她便怎样？

伊阿古 啊，主帅，那时候它就是她的东西了！既然是她的东西，我想她可以把它送给无论什么人的。

奥瑟罗 她的贞操也是她自己的东西，她也可以把它送给无论什么人吗？

伊阿古 她的贞操是一种不可捉摸的品质。世上有几个真正贞洁的妇人？可是讲到那方手帕——

奥瑟罗 天哪，我但愿忘记那句话！你说——啊！它笼罩着我的记忆，就像预兆不祥的乌鸦在染疫人家的屋顶上回旋一样——你说我的手帕在他的手里。

伊阿古 是的，在他手里便怎么样？

奥瑟罗 那可不大好。

IAGO What,
If I had said I had seen him do you wrong?
Or heard him say,—as knaves be such abroad,
Who having, by their own importunate suit,
Or voluntary dotage of some mistress,
Convinced or supplied them, cannot choose
But they must blab—

OTHELLO Hath he said any thing?

IAGO He hath, my lord; but be you well assured,
No more than he'll unswear.

OTHELLO What hath he said?

IAGO 'Faith, that he did—I know not what he did.

OTHELLO What? what?

IAGO Lie—

OTHELLO With her?

IAGO With her, on her; what you will.

OTHELLO Lie with her! lie on her! We say lie on her, when they belie her. Lie with her! that's fulsome.—Handkerchief—confessions—handkerchief!—To confess, and be hanged for his labour;—first, to be hanged, and then to confess.—I tremble at it.

Nature would not invest herself in such shadowing passion without some instruction. It is not words that shake me thus. Pish! Noses, ears, and lips.—Is't possible?—Confess—handkerchief!—O devil!—

Falls in a trance.

IAGO Work on, My medicine, work!
Thus credulous fools are caught;
And many worthy and chaste dames even thus,
All guiltless, meet reproach. What, ho! my lord!
My lord, I say! Othello!

伊阿古 什么！要是我说我看见他干那对不住您的事？或是听见他说——世上尽多那种家伙，他们靠着死命地追求征服了一个女人，或者得到什么情妇的自动的垂青，就禁不住到处向人吹嘘——

奥瑟罗 他说过什么话吗？

伊阿古 说过的，主帅，可是您放心吧，他说过的话，他都可以发誓否认的。

奥瑟罗 他说过什么？

伊阿古 他说，他曾经——我不知道他曾经干些什么事。

奥瑟罗 什么？什么？

伊阿古 跟她睡——

奥瑟罗 在一床？

伊阿古 睡在一床，睡在她的身上；随您怎么说吧。

奥瑟罗 跟她睡在一床！睡在她的身上！我们说睡在她身上，岂不是对她人身的污辱——睡在一床！该死，岂有此理！手帕——口供——手帕！叫他招供了，再把他吊死。先把他吊起来，然后叫他招供。我一想起就气得发抖。人们总是有了某种感应，阴暗的情绪才会笼罩他的心灵；一两句空洞的话是不能给我这样大的震动的。呸！摸鼻子，咬耳朵，吮嘴唇。会有这样的事吗？口供！——手帕！——啊，魔鬼！

晕倒。

伊阿古 显出你的效力来吧，我的妙药，显出你的效力来吧！轻信的愚人是这样落进了圈套；许多贞洁贤淑的娘儿们，都是这样蒙上了不白之冤。喂，主帅！主帅！奥瑟罗！

Enter CASSIO.

IAGO How now, Cassio!
CASSIO What's the matter?
IAGO My lord is fall'n into an epilepsy:
This is his second fit; he had one yesterday.
CASSIO Rub him about the temples.
IAGO No, forbear;
The lethargy must have his quiet course:
If not, he foams at mouth and by and by
Breaks out to savage madness. Look he stirs:
Do you withdraw yourself a little while,
He will recover straight: when he is gone,
I would on great occasion speak with you.

Exit CASSIO.

How is it, general? have you not hurt your head?
OTHELLO Dost thou mock me?
IAGO I mock you! no, by heaven.
Would you would bear your fortune like a man!
OTHELLO A horned man's a monster and a beast.
IAGO There's many a beast then in a populous city,
And many a civil monster.
OTHELLO Did he confess it?
IAGO Good sir, be a man;
Think every bearded fellow that's but yoked
May draw with you: there's millions now alive
That nightly lie in those unproper beds
Which they dare swear peculiar: your case is better.
O, 'tis the spite of hell, the fiend's arch-mock,
To lip a wanton in a secure couch,
And to suppose her chaste! No, let me know;

凯西奥上。

伊阿古 啊，凯西奥！

凯西奥 怎么一回事？

伊阿古 咱们大帅发起癫痫来了。这是他第二次发作，昨天他也发过一次。

凯西奥 在他太阳穴上摩擦摩擦。

伊阿古 不，不行，他这种昏迷状态，必须保持安静！要不然的话，他就要嘴里冒出白沫，慢慢地会发起疯狂来的。瞧！他在动了，你暂时走开一下，他就会恢复原状的。等他走了以后，我还有要紧的话跟你说。

凯西奥下。

怎么啦，主帅？您没有摔痛您的头吧？

奥瑟罗 你在讥笑我吗？

伊阿古 我讥笑您！不，没有这样的事！我愿您像一个大丈夫似的忍受命运的播弄。

奥瑟罗 顶上了绿头巾，还算一个人吗？

伊阿古 在一座热闹的城市里，这种不算人的人多着呢。

奥瑟罗 他自己公然承认了吗？

伊阿古 主帅，您看破一点吧；您只要想一想，哪一个有家室的须眉男子，没有遭到跟您同样命运的可能；世上不知有多少男人，他们的卧榻上容留过无数素昧平生的人，他们自己还满以为这是一块私人的禁地哩。您的情形还不算顶坏。啊！这是最刻毒的恶作剧，魔鬼的最大的玩笑，让一个男人安安心心地搂着枕边的荡妇亲嘴，还以为她是一个三贞九烈的女人！不，我要睁开眼来，先看清自己成了个什么东西，我也就看准了该拿她怎么办。

And knowing what I am, I know what she shall be.

OTHELLO O, thou art wise; 'tis certain.

IAGO Stand you awhile apart;
Confine yourself but in a patient list.
Whilst you were here o'erwhelmed with your grief—
A passion most unsuiting such a man—
Cassio came hither: I shifted him away,
And laid good 'scuse upon your ecstasy,
Bade him anon return and here speak with me;
The which he promised. Do but encave yourself,
And mark the fleers, the gibes, and notable scorns,
That dwell in every region of his face;
For I will make him tell the tale anew,
Where, how, how oft, how long ago, and when
He hath, and is again to cope your wife:
I say, but mark his gesture. Marry, patience;
Or I shall say you are all in all in spleen,
And nothing of a man.

OTHELLO Dost thou hear, Iago?
I will be found most cunning in my patience;
But—dost thou hear?—most bloody.

IAGO That's not amiss;
But yet keep time in all. Will you withdraw?

OTHELLO retires.

Now will I question Cassio of Bianca,
A housewife that by selling her desires
Buys herself bread and clothes: it is a creature
That dotes on Cassio; as 'tis the strumpet's plague
To beguile many and be beguiled by one:
He, when he hears of her, cannot refrain
From the excess of laughter. Here he comes:

奥瑟罗　啊！你是个聪明人，你说得一点不错。

伊阿古　现在请您暂时站在一旁，竭力耐住您的怒气。刚才您恼得昏过去的时候——大人物怎么能这样感情冲动啊——凯西奥曾经到这儿来过；我推说您不省人事是因为一时不舒服，把他打发走了，叫他过一会儿再来跟我谈谈；他已经答应我了。您只要找一处所在躲一躲，就可以看见他满脸得意忘形，冷嘲热讽的神气；因为我要叫他从头叙述他历次跟尊夫人相会的情形，还要问他重温好梦的时间和地点。您留心看看他那副表情吧。可是不要气恼；否则我就要说您一味意气用事，一点没有大丈夫的气概啦。

奥瑟罗　告诉你吧，伊阿古，我会很巧妙地不动声色；可是，你听着，我也会包藏一颗最可怕的杀心。

伊阿古　那很好，可是什么事都要看准时机。您走远一步吧。

奥瑟罗退后。

现在我要向凯西奥谈起比恩卡，一个靠着出卖风情维持生活的雌儿；她热恋着凯西奥；这也是娼妓们的报应，往往她们迷惑了多少的男子，结果却被一个男人迷昏了心。他一听见她的名字，就会忍不住捧腹大笑。他来了。

Re-enter CASSIO.

IAGO As he shall smile, Othello shall go mad;
And his unbookish jealousy must construe
Poor Cassio's smiles, gestures and light behavior,
Quite in the wrong. How do you now, lieutenant?

CASSIO The worser that you give me the addition
Whose want even kills me.

IAGO Ply Desdemona well, and you are sure on't.

Speaking lower.

Now, if this suit lay in Bianca's power,
How quickly should you speed!

CASSIO Alas, poor caitiff!

OTHELLO *[Aside]* Look, how he laughs already!

IAGO I never knew woman love man so.

CASSIO Alas, poor rogue! I think, i' faith, she loves me.

OTHELLO *[Aside]*Now he denies it faintly, and laughs it out.

IAGO Do you hear, Cassio?

OTHELLO *[Aside]*Now he importunes him To tell it o'er: go to; well said, well said.

IAGO She gives it out that you shall marry hey:
Do you intend it?

CASSIO Ha, ha, ha!

OTHELLO *[Aside]*Do you triumph, Roman? do you triumph?

CASSIO I marry her! what? a customer! Prithee, bear some charity to my wit: do not think it so unwholesome.
Ha, ha, ha!

OTHELLO *[Aside]*So, so, so, so: they laugh that win.

IAGO 'Faith, the cry goes that you shall marry her.

CASSIO Prithee, say true.

IAGO I am a very villain else.

凯西奥重上。

伊阿古 他一笑起来，奥瑟罗就会发疯。可怜的凯西奥的嬉笑的神情和轻狂的举止，在他那充满着无知的嫉妒的心头，一定可以引起严重的误会。——您好，副将？

凯西奥 我因为丢掉了这个头衔，正在懊恼得要死，你却还要这样称呼我。

伊阿古 在苔丝狄蒙娜跟前多说几句央求的话，包你原官起用。

低声。

要是这件事情换在比恩卡手里，早就不成问题了。

凯西奥 唉，可怜虫！

奥瑟罗 （旁白）瞧！他已经在笑起来啦！

伊阿古 我从来不知道一个女人会这样爱一个男人。

凯西奥 唉，小东西！我看她倒是真的爱我。

奥瑟罗 （旁白）现在他在含糊否认，想把这事情用一笑搪塞过去。

伊阿古 你听见吗，凯西奥？

奥瑟罗 （旁白）现在他缠住他要他讲一讲经过情形啦。说下去，很好，很好。

伊阿古 她向人家说你将要跟她结婚，你有这个意思吗？

凯西奥 哈哈哈！

奥瑟罗 （旁白）你这样得意吗，好家伙？你这样得意吗？

凯西奥 我跟她结婚！什么？一个卖淫妇？对不起，你不要这样看轻我，我还不至于糊涂到这等地步哩。哈哈哈！

奥瑟罗 （旁白）好，好，好，好。得胜的人才会笑逐颜开。

伊阿古 不骗你，人家都在说你将要跟她结婚。

凯西奥 对不起，别说笑话啦。

伊阿古 我要是骗了你，我就是个大大的混蛋。

OTHELLO *[Aside]*Have you scored me? Well.

CASSIO This is the monkey's own giving out: she is persuaded I will marry her, out of her own love and flattery, not out of my promise.

OTHELLO *[Aside]*Iago beckons me; now he begins the story.

CASSIO She was here even now; she haunts me in every place. I was the other day talking on the sea-bank with certain Venetians; and thither comes the bauble, and, by this hand, she falls me thus about my neck—

OTHELLO *[Aside]*Crying 'O dear Cassio!' as it were: his gesture imports it.

CASSIO So hangs, and lolls, and weeps upon me; so hales, and pulls me: ha, ha, ha!

OTHELLO *[Aside]*Now he tells how she plucked him to my chamber. O, I see that nose of yours, but not that dog I shall throw it to.

CASSIO Well, I must leave her company.

IAGO Before me! look, where she comes.

CASSIO Tis such another fitchew! marry a perfumed one.

Enter BIANCA.

What do you mean by this haunting of me?

BIANCA Let the devil and his dam haunt you! What did you mean by that same handkerchief you gave me even now? I was a fine fool to take it. I must take out the work?— A likely piece of work, that you should find it in your chamber, and not know who left it there! This is some minx's token, and I must take out the work? There; give it your hobby-horse: wheresoever you had it, I'll take out no work on't.

CASSIO How now, my sweet Bianca! how now! how now!

OTHELLO *[Aside]*By heaven, that should be my handkerchief!

BIANCA An you'll come to supper to-night, you may; an you

奥瑟罗　（旁白）你这算是一报还一报吗？好。

凯西奥　一派胡说！她自己一厢情愿，相信我会跟她结婚；我可没有答应她。

奥瑟罗　（旁白）伊阿古在向我打招呼。现在他开始讲他的故事啦。

凯西奥　她刚才还在这儿，她到处缠着我。前天我正在海边跟几个威尼斯人谈话，那傻东西就来啦。不瞒你说，她这样攀住我的颈项——

奥瑟罗　（旁白）叫一声"啊，亲爱的凯西奥！"我可以从他的表情之间猜得出来。

凯西奥　她这样拉住我的衣服，靠在我的怀里，哭个不停，还这样把我拖来拖去，哈哈哈！

奥瑟罗　（旁白）现在他在讲她怎样把他拖到我的寝室里去啦。啊！我看见你的鼻子，可是不知道应该把它丢给哪一条狗吃。

凯西奥　好，我只好离开她。

伊阿古　啊！瞧，她来了。

凯西奥　好一头抹香粉的臭猫！

比恩卡上。

你这样到处盯着我不放，是什么意思呀？

比恩卡　让魔鬼跟他的老娘盯着你吧！你刚才给我的那方手帕算是什么意思？我是个大傻瓜，才会把它收了下来。叫我描下那花样！好看的花手帕可真多哪，居然让你在你的寝室里找到它，却不知道谁把它丢在那边！这一定是哪一个贱丫头送给你的东西，却叫我描下它的花样来！拿去，还给你那个相好吧；随你从什么地方得到这方手帕，我可不高兴描下它的花样。

凯西奥　怎么，我的亲爱的比恩卡！怎么！怎么！

奥瑟罗　（旁白）天哪，那该是我的手帕哩！

比恩卡　今天晚上你要是愿意来吃饭，尽管来吧；要是不愿意来，等你下

will not, come when you are next prepared for.

Exit.

IAGO After her, after her.

CASSIO 'Faith, I must; she'll rail in the street else.

IAGO Will you sup there?

CASSIO 'Faith, I intend so.

IAGO Well, I may chance to see you; for I would very fain speak with you.

CASSIO Prithee, come; will you?

IAGO Go to; say no more.

Exit CASSIO.

OTHELLO *[Advancing]* How shall I murder him, Iago?

IAGO Did you perceive how he laughed at his vice?

OTHELLO O Iago!

IAGO And did you see the handkerchief?

OTHELLO Was that mine?

IAGO Yours by this hand: and to see how he prizes the foolish woman your wife! she gave it him, and he hath given it his whore.

OTHELLO I would have him nine years a-killing.
A fine woman! a fair woman! a sweet woman!

IAGO Nay, you must forget that.

OTHELLO Ay, let her rot, and perish, and be damned to-night;
for she shall not live: no, my heart is turned to
stone; I strike it, and it hurts my hand. O, the
world hath not a sweeter creature: she might lie by
an emperor's side and command him tasks.

IAGO Nay, that's not your way.

OTHELLO Hang her! I do but say what she is: so delicate with her

回有兴致的时候再来吧。

下。

伊 阿 古 追上去，追上去。

凯 西 奥 真的，我必须追上去，否则她会沿街谩骂的。

伊 阿 古 你预备到她家里去吃饭吗？

凯 西 奥 是的，我想去。

伊 阿 古 好，也许我会再碰见你，因为我很想跟你谈谈。

凯 西 奥 请你一定来吧。

伊 阿 古 得啦，别多说啦。

凯西奥下。

奥 瑟 罗 （趋前）伊阿古，我应该怎样杀死他？

伊 阿 古 您看见他一听到人家提起他的丑事，就笑得多么高兴吗？

奥 瑟 罗 啊，伊阿古！

伊 阿 古 您还看见那方手帕吗？

奥 瑟 罗 那就是我的吗？

伊 阿 古 我可以举手起誓，那是您的。瞧他多么看得起您那位痴心的太太！她把手帕送给他，他却拿去给了他的娼妇。

奥 瑟 罗 我要用九年的时间慢慢地磨死她。一个高雅的女人！一个美貌的女人！一个温柔的女人！

伊 阿 古 不，您必须忘掉那些。

奥 瑟 罗 嗯，让她今夜腐烂、死亡、堕入地狱吧，因为她不能再活在世上。不，我的心已经变成铁石了；我打它，反而打痛了我的手。啊！世上没有一个比她更可爱的东西；她可以睡在一个皇帝的身边，命令他干无论什么事。

伊 阿 古 您素来不是这个样子的。

奥 瑟 罗 让她死吧！我不过说她是怎么样的一个人。她的针线活儿是这样

needle: an admirable musician: O! she will sing the savageness out of a bear: of so high and plenteous wit and invention:—

IAGO She's the worse for all this.

OTHELLO O, a thousand thousand times: and then, of so gentle a condition!

IAGO Ay, too gentle.

OTHELLO Nay, that's certain: but yet the pity of it, Iago!
O Iago, the pity of it, Iago!

IAGO If you are so fond over her iniquity, give her patent to offend; for, if it touch not you, it comes near nobody.

OTHELLO I will chop her into messes: cuckold me!

IAGO O, 'tis foul in her.

OTHELLO With mine officer!

IAGO That's fouler.

OTHELLO Get me some poison, Iago; this night: I'll not expostulate with her, lest her body and beauty unprovide my mind again: this night, Iago.

IAGO Do it not with poison, strangle her in her bed, even the bed she hath contaminated.

OTHELLO Good, good: the justice of it pleases: very good.

IAGO And for Cassio, let me be his undertaker: you shall hear more by midnight.

OTHELLO Excellent good.

A trumpet within.

What trumpet is that same?

IAGO Something from Venice, sure. 'Tis Lodovico
Come from the duke: and, see, your wife is with him.

Enter LODOVICO, DESDEMONA, and Attendants

精妙！一个出色的音乐家！啊，她唱起歌来，可以驯服一头野熊的心！她的心思才智，又是这样敏慧多能！

伊阿古 唯其这样多才多艺，干出这种丑事来，才格外叫人气恼。

奥瑟罗 啊！一千倍、一千倍的可恼！而且她的性格又是这样温柔！

伊阿古 嗯，太温柔了。

奥瑟罗 对啦，一点不错。可是，伊阿古，可惜！啊！伊阿古！伊阿古！太可惜啦！

伊阿古 要是您对于一个失节之妇，还是这样恋恋不舍，那么索性采取放任吧。因为既然您自己也不以为意，当然更不干别人的事。

奥瑟罗 我要把她剁成一堆肉酱。叫我当一个王八！

伊阿古 啊，她太不顾羞耻啦！

奥瑟罗 跟我的部将通奸！

伊阿古 那尤其可恶。

奥瑟罗 给我弄些毒药来，伊阿古，今天晚上。我不想跟她多费唇舌，免得她的肉体和美貌再打动了我的心。今天晚上，伊阿古。

伊阿古 不要用毒药，在她床上扼死她，就在那被她玷污了的床上。

奥瑟罗 好，好，那是一个大快人心的处置，很好。

伊阿古 至于凯西奥，让我去取他的命吧。您在午夜前后，一定可以听到消息。

奥瑟罗 好极了。

内喇叭声。

那是什么喇叭的声音？

伊阿古 一定是从威尼斯来了什么人。——是罗多维科奉公爵之命到这儿来了。瞧，您那位太太也跟他在一起。

罗多维科、苔丝狄蒙娜及侍从等上。

LODOVICO Save you, worthy general!

OTHELLO With all my heart, sir.

LODOVICO The duke and senators of Venice greet you.

Gives him a letter.

OTHELLO I kiss the instrument of their pleasures.

Opens the letter, and reads.

DESDEMONA And what's the news, good cousin Lodovico?

IAGO I am very glad to see you, signior
Welcome to Cyprus.

LODOVICO I thank you. How does Lieutenant Cassio?

IAGO Lives, sir.

DESDEMONA Cousin, there's fall'n between him and my lord An unkind breach: but you shall make all well.

OTHELLO Are you sure of that?

DESDEMONA My lord?

OTHELLO *[Reads]* 'This fail you not to do, as you will—'

LODOVICO He did not call; he's busy in the paper.
Is there division 'twixt my lord and Cassio?

DESDEMONA A most unhappy one: I would do much
To atone them, for the love I bear to Cassio.

OTHELLO Fire and brimstone!

DESDEMONA My lord?

OTHELLO Are you wise?

DESDEMONA What, is he angry?

LODOVICO May be the letter moved him;
For, as I think, they do command him home,
Deputing Cassio in his government.

DESDEMONA Trust me, I am glad on't.

OTHELLO Indeed!

罗多维科 上帝保佑您，尊贵的将军！

奥瑟罗 祝福您，大人。

罗多维科 公爵和威尼斯的元老们问候您安好。

以信交奥瑟罗。

奥瑟罗 我敬吻他们的恩命。

拆信阅读。

苔丝狄蒙娜 罗多维科大哥，威尼斯有什么消息？

伊阿古 我很高兴看见您，大人，欢迎您到塞浦路斯来！

罗多维科 谢谢。凯西奥副将好吗？

伊阿古 他还健在，大人。

苔丝狄蒙娜 大哥，他跟我的丈夫闹了点儿别扭；可是您可以使他们言归于好。

奥瑟罗 你有把握吗？

苔丝狄蒙娜 您怎么说，我的主？

奥瑟罗 （读信）“务必照办为要，不得有误。——”

罗多维科 他没有回答，他正在忙着读信。将军跟凯西奥果然有了意见吗？

苔丝狄蒙娜 有了很不幸的意见；为了我对凯西奥所抱的好感，我很愿意尽力调解他们。

奥瑟罗 该死！

苔丝狄蒙娜 您怎么说，我的主？

奥瑟罗 你聪明吗？

苔丝狄蒙娜 什么！他生气了吗？

罗多维科 也许这封信激动了他。因为照我猜想起来，他们是要召他回国，叫凯西奥代理他的职务。

苔丝狄蒙娜 真的吗？那好极了。

奥瑟罗 当真！

DESDEMONA My lord?

OTHELLO I am glad to see you mad.

DESDEMONA Why, sweet Othello,—

OTHELLO *[Striking her]* Devil!

DESDEMONA I have not deserved this.

LODOVICO My lord, this would not be believed in Venice,
Though I should swear I saw't: 'tis very much:
Make her amends; she weeps.

OTHELLO O devil, devil!
If that the earth could teem with woman's tears,
Each drop she falls would prove a crocodile.
Out of my sight!

DESDEMONA I will not stay to offend you.

Going.

LODOVICO Truly, an obedient lady:
I do beseech your lordship, call her back.

OTHELLO Mistress!

DESDEMONA My lord?

OTHELLO What would you with her, sir?

LODOVICO Who, I, my lord?

OTHELLO Ay; you did wish that I would make her turn:
Sir, she can turn, and turn, and yet go on,
And turn again; and she can weep, sir, weep;
And she's obedient, as you say, obedient,
Very obedient. Proceed you in your tears.
Concerning this, sir,—O well-painted passion!—
I am commanded home. Get you away;
I'll send for you anon. Sir, I obey the mandate,
And will return to Venice. Hence, avaunt!

Exit DESDEMONA.

苔丝狄蒙娜 您怎么说，我的主？

奥瑟罗 你要是发了疯，我才高兴。

苔丝狄蒙娜 为什么，亲爱的奥瑟罗？

奥瑟罗 魔鬼！（击苔丝狄蒙娜）

苔丝狄蒙娜 我没有错处，您不该这样对待我。

罗多维科 将军，我要是把这回事情告诉威尼斯人，即使发誓说我亲眼看见，他们也一定不会相信我。这太过分了，向她赔罪吧，她在哭了。

奥瑟罗 啊，魔鬼！魔鬼！要是妇人的眼泪有孳生化育的力量，她的每一滴泪，掉在地上，都会变成一条鳄鱼。走开，不要让我看见你！

苔丝狄蒙娜 我不愿留在这儿害您生气。

欲去。

罗多维科 真是一位顺从的夫人。将军，请您叫她回来吧。

奥瑟罗 夫人！

苔丝狄蒙娜 我的主？

奥瑟罗 大人，您要跟她说些什么话？

罗多维科 谁？我吗，将军？

奥瑟罗 嗯，您要我叫她转来，现在她转过来了。她会转来转去，走一步路回一个身；她还会哭，大人，她还会哭；她是非常顺从的，正像您所说，非常顺从。尽管流你的眼泪吧。大人，这信上的意思——好一股装腔作势的劲儿！——是要叫我回去——你去吧，等会儿我再叫人来唤你——大人，我服从他们的命令，不日就可以束装上路，回到威尼斯去——去！滚开！

苔丝狄蒙娜下。

Cassio shall have my place. And, sir, tonight,
I do entreat that we may sup together:
You are welcome, sir, to Cyprus.—Goats and monkeys!

Exit.

LODOVICO Is this the noble Moor whom our full senate
Call all in all sufficient? Is this the nature
Whom passion could not shake? whose solid virtue
The shot of accident, nor dart of chance,
Could neither graze nor pierce?

IAGO He is much changed.

LODOVICO Are his wits safe? is he not light of brain?

IAGO He's that he is: I may not breathe my censure
What he might be: if what he might he is not,
I would to heaven he were!

LODOVICO What, strike his wife!

IAGO 'Faith, that was not so well; yet would I knew
That stroke would prove the worst!

LODOVICO Is it his use?
Or did the letters work upon his blood,
And new-create this fault?

IAGO Alas, alas!
It is not honesty in me to speak
What I have seen and known. You shall observe him,
And his own courses will denote him so
That I may save my speech: do but go after,
And mark how he continues.

LODOVICO I am sorry that I am deceived in him.

Exeunt.

凯西奥可以接替我的位置。今天晚上，大人，我还要请您赏光便饭。欢迎您到塞浦路斯来！——山羊和猴子！

下。

罗多维科 这就是为我们整个元老院所同声赞叹、称为全才全德的那位英勇的摩尔人吗？这就是那喜怒之情不能把它震撼的高贵的天性吗？那命运的箭矢不能把它擦伤穿破的坚定的德操吗？

伊阿古 他已经大大变了样子啦。

罗多维科 他的头脑没有毛病吗？他的神经是不是有点错乱？

伊阿古 他就是他那个样子，我实在不敢说他还会变成怎么一个样子。如果他不是像他所应该的那样，那么但愿他也不至于这个样子！

罗多维科 什么！打他的妻子！

伊阿古 真的，那可不大好。可是我但愿知道他对她没有比这更暴虐的行为！

罗多维科 他一向都是这样的吗？还是因为信上的话激怒了他，才会有这种以前所没有的过失？

伊阿古 唉！唉！按着我的地位，我实在不便把我所看见所知道的一切说出口来。您不妨留心注意他，他自己的行动就可以说明一切，用不着我多说了。请您跟上去，看他还会做出什么花样来。

罗多维科 他竟是这样一个人，真使我大失所望啊。

同下。

SCENE II

A room in the castle.
Enter OTHELLO and EMILIA.

OTHELLO You have seen nothing then?
EMILIA Nor ever heard, nor ever did suspect.
OTHELLO Yes, you have seen Cassio and she together.
EMILIA But then I saw no harm, and then I heard
Each syllable that breath made up between them.
OTHELLO What, did they never whisper?
EMILIA Never, my lord.
OTHELLO Nor send you out o' the way?
EMILIA Never.
OTHELLO To fetch her fan, her gloves, her mask, nor nothing?
EMILIA Never, my lord.
OTHELLO That's strange.
EMILIA I durst, my lord, to wager she is honest,
Lay down my soul at stake: if you think other,
Remove your thought; it doth abuse your bosom.
If any wretch have put this in your head,
Let heaven requite it with the serpent's curse!
For, if she be not honest, chaste, and true,
There's no man happy; the purest of their wives
Is foul as slander.
OTHELLO Bid her come hither: go.

Exit EMILIA.

She says enough; yet she's a simple bawd
That cannot say as much. This is a subtle whore,
A closet lock and key of villanous secrets
And yet she'll kneel and pray; I have seen her do't.

Enter DESDEMONA with EMILIA.

第二场

城堡中一室。
奥瑟罗及爱米利娅上。

奥瑟罗 那么你没有看见什么吗？

爱米利娅 没有看见，没有听见，也没有疑心到。

奥瑟罗 你不是看见凯西奥跟她在一起吗？

爱米利娅 可是我不知道那有什么不对，而且我听见他们两人所说的每一个字。

奥瑟罗 什么！他们从来不曾低声耳语吗？

爱米利娅 从来没有，将军。

奥瑟罗 也不曾打发你走开吗？

爱米利娅 没有。

奥瑟罗 没有叫你去替她拿扇子、手套、脸罩，或是什么东西吗？

爱米利娅 没有，将军。

奥瑟罗 那可奇怪了。

爱米利娅 将军，我敢用我的灵魂打赌她是贞洁的。要是您疑心她有非礼的行为，赶快除掉这种思想吧，因为那是您心理上的一个污点。要是哪一个混蛋把这种思想放进您的脑袋里，让上天罚他变成一条蛇，受永远的诅咒！假如她不是贞洁、贤淑和忠诚的，那么世上没有一个幸福的男人了；最纯洁的妻子，也会变成最丑恶的淫妇。

奥瑟罗 叫她到这儿来，去。

爱米利娅下。

她的话说得很动听；可是这种拉惯皮条的人，都是天生的利嘴。这是一个狡猾的淫妇，一肚子千刁万恶，当着人却会跪下来向天祈祷。我看见过她这一种手段。

爱米利娅偕苔丝狄蒙娜重上。

DESDEMONA My lord, what is your will?
OTHELLO Pray, chuck, come hither.
DESDEMONA What is your pleasure?
OTHELLO Let me see your eyes;
Look in my face.
DESDEMONA What horrible fancy's this?
OTHELLO *[To EMILIA]* Some of your function, mistress;
Leave procreants alone and shut the door;
Cough, or cry 'hem,' if any body come:
Your mystery, your mystery: nay, dispatch.

Exit EMILIA.

DESDEMONA Upon my knees, what doth your speech import?
I understand a fury in your words.
But not the words.
OTHELLO Why, what art thou?
DESDEMONA Your wife, my lord; your true
And loyal wife.
OTHELLO Come, swear it, damn thyself
Lest, being like one of heaven, the devils themselves
Should fear to seize thee: therefore be double damn'd:
Swear thou art honest.
DESDEMONA Heaven doth truly know it.
OTHELLO Heaven truly knows that thou art false as hell.
DESDEMONA To whom, my lord? with whom? how am I false?

OTHELLO O Desdemona! away! away! away!
DESDEMONA Alas the heavy day! Why do you weep?
Am I the motive of these tears, my lord?
If haply you my father do suspect
An instrument of this your calling back,
Lay not your blame on me: If you have lost him,

苔丝狄蒙娜 我的主，您有什么吩咐？

奥瑟罗 过来，乖乖。

苔丝狄蒙娜 您要我怎么样？

奥瑟罗 让我看看你的眼睛。瞧着我的脸。

苔丝狄蒙娜 这是什么古怪的念头？

奥瑟罗 （向爱米利娅）你去留心你的事吧，奶奶，把门关了，让我们两人在这儿谈谈心。要是有人来了，你就在门口咳嗽一声。干你的贵营生去吧，快，快！

爱米利娅下。

苔丝狄蒙娜 我跪在您的面前，请您告诉我您这些话是什么意思？我知道您在生气，可是我不懂您的话。

奥瑟罗 嘿，你是什么人？

苔丝狄蒙娜 我的主，我是您的妻子，您的忠贞不二的妻子。

奥瑟罗 来，发一个誓，让你自己死后下地狱吧。因为你的外表太像一个天使了，倘不是在不贞之上，再加一重伪誓的罪名，也许魔鬼们会不敢抓你下去的，所以发誓说你是贞洁的吧。

苔丝狄蒙娜 天知道我是贞洁的。

奥瑟罗 天知道你是像地狱一样淫邪的。

苔丝狄蒙娜 我的主，我对谁干了欺心的事？我跟哪一个人有不端的行为？我怎么是淫邪的？

奥瑟罗 啊，苔丝狄蒙娜！去！去！去！

苔丝狄蒙娜 唉，不幸的日子！——您为什么哭？您的眼泪是为我而流的吗，我的主？要是您疑心这次奉召回国，是我父亲的主意，请您不要怪我；您固然失去他的好感，我也已经失去他的慈爱了。

Why, I have lost him too.

OTHELLO Had it pleased heaven
To try me with affliction; had they rain'd
All kinds of sores and shames on my bare head.
Steep'd me in poverty to the very lips,
Given to captivity me and my utmost hopes,
I should have found in some place of my soul
A drop of patience: but, alas, to make me
A fixed figure for the time of scorn
To point his slow unmoving finger at!
Yet could I bear that too; well, very well:
But there, where I have garner'd up my heart,
Where either I must live, or bear no life;
The fountain from the which my current runs,
Or else dries up; to be discarded thence!
Or keep it as a cistern for foul toads
To knot and gender in! Turn thy complexion there,
Patience, thou young and rose-lipp'd cherubin,—
Ay, there, look grim as hell!

DESDEMONA I hope my noble lord esteems me honest.

OTHELLO O, ay; as summer flies are in the shambles,
That quicken even with blowing. O thou weed,
Who art so lovely fair and smell'st so sweet
That the sense aches at thee, would thou hadst ne'er been born!

DESDEMONA Alas, what ignorant sin have I committed?

OTHELLO Was this fair paper, this most goodly book,
Made to write 'whore' upon? What committed!
Committed! O thou public commoner!
I should make very forges of my cheeks,
That would to cinders burn up modesty,

奥瑟罗　要是上天的意思，要让我受尽种种的折磨；要是他用诸般的痛苦和耻辱降在我的毫无防卫的头上，把我浸没在贫困的泥沼里，剥夺我的一切自由和希望，我也可以在我的灵魂的一隅之中，找到一滴忍耐的甘露。可是唉！在这尖酸刻薄的世上，做一个被人戟指笑骂的目标！就连这个，我也完全可以容忍。可是我的心灵失去了归宿，我的生命失去了寄托，我的活力的源泉枯竭了，变成了蛤蟆繁育生息的污池！忍耐，你朱唇韶颜的天婴啊，转变你的脸色，让它化成地狱般的狰狞吧！

苔丝狄蒙娜　我希望我在我的尊贵的夫主眼中，是一个贤良贞洁的妻子。

奥瑟罗　啊，是的，就像夏天肉铺里的苍蝇一样贞洁——一边撒它的卵子，一边就在受孕。你这野草闲花啊！你的颜色是这样娇美，你的香气是这样芬芳，人家看见你嗅到你就会心疼；但愿世上从来不曾有过你！

苔丝狄蒙娜　唉！我究竟犯了什么连我自己也不知道的罪恶呢？

奥瑟罗　这一张皎洁的白纸，这一本美丽的书册，是要让人家写上“娼妓”两个字的吗？犯了什么罪恶！啊，你这人尽可夫的娼妇！我只要一说起你所干的事，我的两颊就会变成两座熔炉，把“廉耻”烧为灰烬。犯了什么罪恶！天神见了它要掩鼻而过；月亮看见了要羞得闭上眼睛；碰见什么都要亲吻的淫荡的风，也静悄悄地躲在岩窟里面，不愿听见人家提起它的名字。犯了什么罪恶！

Did I but speak thy deeds. What committed!
Heaven stops the nose at it and the moon winks,
The bawdy wind that kisses all it meets
Is hush'd within the hollow mine of earth,
And will not hear it. What committed!
Impudent strumpet!

DESDEMONA By heaven, you do me wrong.

OTHELLO Are you not a strumpet?

DESDEMONA No, as I am a Christian:
If to preserve this vessel for my lord
From any other foul unlawful touch
Be not to be a strumpet, I am none.

OTHELLO What, not a whore?

DESDEMONA No, as I shall be saved.

OTHELLO Is't possible?

DESDEMONA O, heaven forgive us!

OTHELLO I cry you mercy, then:
I took you for that cunning whore of Venice
That married with Othello.
Raising his voice
You, mistress,
That have the office opposite to Saint Peter,
And keep the gate of hell!

Re-enter EMILIA.

OTHELLO You, you, ay, you!
We have done our course; there's money for your pains:
I pray you, turn the key and keep our counsel.

Exit.

EMILIA Alas, what does this gentleman conceive?

不要脸的娼妇！

苔丝狄蒙娜　天啊，您不该这样侮辱我！

奥瑟罗　你不是一个娼妇吗？

苔丝狄蒙娜　不，我发誓我不是，否则我就不是一个基督徒。要是为我的主保持这一个清白的身子，不让淫邪的手把它污毁，要是这样的行为可以使我免去娼妇的恶名，那么我就不是娼妇。

奥瑟罗　什么！你不是一个娼妇吗？

苔丝狄蒙娜　不，否则我死后没有得救的希望。

奥瑟罗　真的吗？

苔丝狄蒙娜　啊！上天饶恕我们！

奥瑟罗　那么我真是多多冒昧了；我还以为你就是那个嫁给奥瑟罗的威尼斯的狡猾的娼妇哩。——喂，你这位刚刚和圣彼得干着相反的差使的，看守地狱门户的奶奶！

爱米利娅重上。

奥瑟罗　你，你，对了，你！我们已经完事了。这几个钱是给你作为酬劳的；请你开了门上的锁，不要泄漏我们的秘密。

下。

爱米利娅　唉！这位老爷究竟在转些什么念头呀？您怎么啦，夫人？您怎

How do you, madam? how do you, my good lady?

DESDEMONA 'Faith, half asleep.

EMILIA Good madam, what's the matter with my lord?

DESDEMONA With who?

EMILIA Why, with my lord, madam.

DESDEMONA Who is thy lord?

EMILIA He that is yours, sweet lady.

DESDEMONA I have none: do not talk to me, Emilia;
I cannot weep; nor answer have I none,
But what should go by water. Prithee, tonight
Lay on my bed my wedding sheets: remember;
And call thy husband hither.

EMILIA Here's a change indeed!

Exit.

DESDEMONA 'Tis meet I should be used so, very meet.
How have I been behaved, that he might stick
The small'st opinion on my least misuse?

Re-enter EMILIA with IAGO.

IAGO What is your pleasure, madam?
How is't with you?

DESDEMONA I cannot tell. Those that do teach young babes
Do it with gentle means and easy tasks:
He might have chid me so; for, in good faith,
I am a child to chiding.

IAGO What's the matter, lady?

EMILIA Alas, Iago, my lord hath so bewhor'd her.
Thrown such despite and heavy terms upon her,
As true hearts cannot bear.

DESDEMONA Am I that name, Iago?

IAGO What name, fair lady?

么啦，我的好夫人？

苔丝狄蒙娜　我是在半醒半睡之中。

爱米利娅　好夫人，我的主到底有些什么心事？

苔丝狄蒙娜　谁？

爱米利娅　我的主呀，夫人。

苔丝狄蒙娜　谁是你的主？

爱米利娅　我的主就是你的丈夫，好夫人。

苔丝狄蒙娜　我没有丈夫。不要对我说话，爱米利娅；我不能哭，我没有话可以回答你，除了我的眼泪。请你今夜把我结婚的被褥铺在我的床上，记好了；再去替我叫你的丈夫来。

爱米利娅　真是变了，变了！

下。

苔丝狄蒙娜　我应该受到这样的待遇，全然是应该的。我究竟有些什么不检的行为——哪怕只是一丁点儿的错误，才会引起他的猜疑呢？

爱米利娅率伊阿古重上。

伊阿古　夫人，您有什么吩咐？您怎么啦？

苔丝狄蒙娜　我不知道。小孩子做了错事，做父母的总是用温和的态度，轻微的责罚教训他们。他也可以这样责备我，因为我是一个该受管教的孩子。

伊阿古　怎么一回事，夫人？

爱米利娅　唉！伊阿古，将军口口声声骂她娼妇，用那样难堪的名字加在她的身上，稍有人心的人，谁听见了都不能忍受。

苔丝狄蒙娜　我应该得到那样一个称呼吗，伊阿古？

伊阿古　什么称呼，好夫人？

DESDEMONA Such as she says my lord did say I was.

EMILIA He call'd her whore: a beggar in his drink
Could not have laid such terms upon his callat.

IAGO Why did he so?

DESDEMONA I do not know; I am sure I am none such.

IAGO Do not weep, do not weep. Alas the day!

EMILIA Hath she forsook so many noble matches,
Her father and her country and her friends,
To be call'd whore? would it not make one weep?

DESDEMONA It is my wretched fortune.

IAGO Beshrew him for't!
How comes this trick upon him?

DESDEMONA Nay, heaven doth know.

EMILIA I will be hang'd, if some eternal villain,
Some busy and insinuating rogue,
Some cogging, cozening slave, to get some office,
Have not devised this slander; I'll be hang'd else.

IAGO Fie, there is no such man; it is impossible.

DESDEMONA If any such there be, heaven pardon him!

EMILIA A halter pardon him! and hell gnaw his bones!
Why should he call her whore? who keeps her company?
What place? what time? what form? what likelihood?
The Moor's abused by some most villanous knave,
Some base notorious knave, some scurvy fellow.
O heaven, that such companions thou'dst unfold,
And put in every honest hand a whip
To lash the rascals naked through the world
Even from the east to the west!

IAGO Speak within door.

EMILIA O, fie upon them! Some such squire he was
That turn'd your wit the seamy side without,
And made you to suspect me with the Moor.

苔丝狄蒙娜 就像她说我的主称呼我的那种名字。

爱米利娅 他叫她娼妇。一个喝醉了酒的叫花子，也不会把这种名字加在他的姘妇身上。

伊阿古 为什么他要这样？

苔丝狄蒙娜 我不知道，我相信我不是那样的女人。

伊阿古 不要哭，不要哭。唉！

爱米利娅 多少名门贵族向她求婚，她都拒绝了；她抛下了老父，离乡背井，远别亲友，结果却只讨他骂一声娼妇吗？这还不叫人伤心吗？

苔丝狄蒙娜 都是我自己命薄。

伊阿古 他太岂有此理了！他怎么会起这种心思的？

苔丝狄蒙娜 天才知道。

爱米利娅 我可以打赌，一定有一个万劫不复的恶人，一个爱管闲事、鬼讨好的家伙，一个说假话骗人的奴才，因为要想钻求差使，造出这样的谣言来；要是我的话说得不对，我愿意让人家把我吊死。

伊阿古 呸！哪里有这样的人？一定不会的。

苔丝狄蒙娜 要是果然有这样的人，愿上天宽恕他！

爱米利娅 宽恕他！一条绳子箍住他的颈项，地狱里的恶鬼咬碎他的骨头！他为什么叫她娼妇？谁跟她在一起？什么所在？什么时候？什么方式？什么根据？这摩尔人一定是上了不知哪一个千刁万恶的坏人的当，一个下流的大混蛋，一个卑鄙的家伙！天啊！愿你揭破这种家伙的嘴脸，让每一个老实人的手里都拿一根鞭子，把这些混蛋们脱光了衣服抽一顿，从东方一直抽到西方！

伊阿古 别嚷得给外边都听见了。

爱米利娅 哼，可恶的东西！前回弄昏了你的头，使你疑心我跟这摩尔人有暧昧的，也就是这种家伙。

IAGO You are a fool; go to.

DESDEMONA O good Iago,
What shall I do to win my lord again?
Good friend, go to him; for, by this light of heaven,
I know not how I lost him. Here I kneel:
If e'er my will did trespass 'gainst his love,
Either in discourse of thought or actual deed,
Or that mine eyes, mine ears, or any sense,
Delighted them in any other form;
Or that I do not yet, and ever did.
And ever will—though he do shake me off
To beggarly divorcement—love him dearly,
Comfort forswear me! Unkindness may do much;
And his unkindness may defeat my life,
But never taint my love. I cannot say 'whore:'
It does abhor me now I speak the word;
To do the act that might the addition earn
Not the world's mass of vanity could make me.

IAGO I pray you, be content; 'tis but his humour:
The business of the state does him offence,
And he does chide with you.

DESDEMONA If 'twere no other—

IAGO 'Tis but so, I warrant.

Trumpets within.

Hark, how these instruments summon to supper!
The messengers of Venice stay the meat;
Go in, and weep not; all things shall be well.

Exeunt DESDEMONA and EMILIA.
Enter RODERIGO.

IAGO How now, Roderigo!

RODERIGO I do not find that thou dealest justly with me.

伊 阿 古 好了，好了，你是个傻瓜。

苔丝狄蒙娜 好伊阿古啊，我应当怎样重新取得我的丈夫的欢心呢？好朋友，替我向他解释解释。因为凭着天上的太阳起誓，我实在不知道我怎么会失去他的宠爱。我对天下跪，要是在思想上、行动上，我曾经有意背弃他的爱情；要是我的眼睛、我的耳朵或是我的任何感觉，曾经对别人发生爱悦；要是我在过去、现在和将来，不是那样始终深深地爱着他，即使他把我弃如敝屣，也不因此而改变我对他的忠诚；要是我果然有那样的过失，愿我终身不能享受快乐的日子！无情可以给人重大的打击；他的无情也许会摧残我的生命，可是永不能毁坏我的爱情。我不愿提起“娼妇”两个字，一说到它就会使我心生憎恶，更不用说亲自去干那博得这种丑名的勾当了；整个世界的荣华也不能诱动我。

伊 阿 古 请您宽心，这不过是他一时的心绪恶劣，在国家大事方面受了点刺激，所以跟您怄起气来啦。

苔丝狄蒙娜 要是没有别的原因——

伊 阿 古 只是为了这个原因，我可以保证。

喇叭声。

听！喇叭在吹晚餐的信号了；威尼斯的使者在等候进餐。进去，不要哭，一切都会圆满解决的。

苔丝狄蒙娜、爱米利娅下。
罗德利哥上。

伊 阿 古 啊，罗德利哥！

罗德利哥 我看你全然在欺骗我。

IAGO What in the contrary?

RODERIGO Every day thou daffest me with some device, Iago; and rather, as it seems to me now, keepest from me all conveniency than suppliest me with the least advantage of hope. I will indeed no longer endure it, nor am I yet persuaded to put up in peace what already I have foolishly suffered.

IAGO Will you hear me, Roderigo?

RODERIGO 'Faith, I have heard too much, for your words and performances are no kin together.

IAGO You charge me most unjustly.

RODERIGO With nought but truth. I have wasted myself out of my means. The jewels you have had from me to deliver to Desdemona would half have corrupted a votarist: you have told me she hath received them and returned me expectations and comforts of sudden respect and acquaintance, but I find none.

IAGO Well; go to; very well.

RODERIGO Very well! go to! I cannot go to, man; nor 'tis not very well: nay, I think it is scurvy, and begin to find myself fobbed in it.

IAGO Very well.

RODERIGO I tell you 'tis not very well. I will make myself known to Desdemona: if she will return me my jewels, I will give over my suit and repent my unlawful solicitation; if not, assure yourself I will seek satisfaction of you.

IAGO You have said now.

RODERIGO Ay, and said nothing but what I protest intendment of doing.

IAGO Why, now I see there's mettle in thee, and even from this instant to build on thee a better opinion than ever before. Give me thy hand, Roderigo: thou hast taken against me a most just exception; but yet, I protest, I have dealt most directly in thy affair.

RODERIGO It hath not appeared.

IAGO I grant indeed it hath not appeared, and your suspicion is

伊 阿 古 我怎么欺骗你？

罗德利哥 伊阿古，你每天在我面前要手段，把我支吾过去。照我现在看来，你非但不给我开一线方便之门，反而使我的希望一天小似一天。我实在再也忍不住了。为了自己的愚蠢，我已经吃了不少的苦头，这一笔账我也不能就此善罢甘休。

伊 阿 古 你愿意听我说吗，罗德利哥？

罗德利哥 哼，我已经听得太多了。你的话和行动是不相符合的。

伊 阿 古 你太冤枉人啦。

罗德利哥 我一点没有冤枉你。我的钱都花光啦。你从我手里拿去送给苔丝狄蒙娜的珠宝，即使一个圣徒也会被它诱惑的；你对我说她已经收下了，告诉我不久就可以听到喜讯，可是到现在还不见一点动静。

伊 阿 古 好，算了，很好。

罗德利哥 很好！算了！我不能就此算了，朋友，这事情也不很好。我举手起誓，这种手段太卑鄙了；我开始觉得我自己受了骗了。

伊 阿 古 很好。

罗德利哥 我告诉你这事情不很好。我要亲自去见苔丝狄蒙娜，要是她肯把我的珠宝还我，我愿意死了这片心，忏悔我这种非礼的追求；要不然的话，你留心点儿吧，我一定要跟你算账。

伊 阿 古 你现在话说完了吧？

罗德利哥 喂，我的话都是说过就做的。

伊 阿 古 好，现在我才知道你是一个有骨气的人；从这一刻起，你已经使我比从前加倍看重你了。把你的手给我，罗德利哥。你责备我的话，都非常有理；可是我还要声明一句，我替你干这件事情，的的确确是尽忠竭力，不敢昧一分良心的。

罗德利哥 那还没有事实的证明。

伊 阿 古 我承认还没有事实的证明，你的疑心不是没有理由的。可是，罗

not without wit and judgment. But,
Roderigo, if thou hast that in thee indeed, which I have greater reason to believe now than ever, I mean purpose, courage and valour, this night show it: if thou the next night following enjoy not Desdemona, take me from this world with treachery and devise engines for my life.

RODERIGO Well, what is it? is it within reason and compass?

IAGO Sir, there is especial commission come from Venice to depute Cassio in Othello's place.

RODERIGO Is that true? why, then Othello and Desdemona return again to Venice.

IAGO O, no; he goes into Mauritania and takes away with him the fair Desdemona, unless his abode be lingered here by some accident: wherein none can be so determinate as the removing of Cassio.

RODERIGO How do you mean, removing of him?

IAGO Why, by making him uncapable of Othello's place; knocking out his brains.

RODERIGO And that you would have me to do?

IAGO Ay, if you dare do yourself a profit and a right. He sups to-night with a harlotry, and thither will I go to him: he knows not yet of his honourable fortune. If you will watch his going thence, which I will fashion to fall out between twelve and one, you may take him at your pleasure: I will be near to second your attempt, and he shall fall between us. Come, stand not amazed at it, but go along with me; I will show you such a necessity in his death that you shall think yourself bound to put it on him. It is now high suppertime, and the night grows to waste: about it.

RODERIGO I will hear further reason for this.

IAGO And you shall be satisfied.

Exeunt.

德利哥，要是你果然有决心，有勇气，有胆量——我现在相信你一定有的——今晚你就可以表现出来；要是明天夜里你不能享用苔丝狄蒙娜，你可以用无论什么恶毒的手段、什么阴险的计谋，取去我的生命。

罗德利哥 好，你要我怎么干？是说得通做得到的事吗？

伊阿古 老兄，威尼斯已经派了专使来，叫凯西奥代替奥瑟罗的职位。

罗德利哥 真的吗？那么奥瑟罗和苔丝狄蒙娜都要回到威尼斯去了。

伊阿古 啊，不，他要到毛里塔尼亚去，把那美丽的苔丝狄蒙娜一起带走，除非这儿出了什么事，使他耽搁下来。最好的办法是把凯西奥除掉。

罗德利哥 你说把他除掉是什么意思？

伊阿古 砸碎他的脑袋，让他不能担任奥瑟罗的职位。

罗德利哥 那就是你要我去干的事吗？

伊阿古 嗯，要是你敢做一件对你自己有利益的事。他今晚在一个妓女家里吃饭，我也要到那儿去见他。现在他还没有知道他自己的命运。我可以设法让他在十二点钟到一点钟之间从那儿出来，你只要留心在门口守候，就可以照你的意思把他处置；我就在附近接应你，他在我们两人之间一定逃不了。来，不要发呆，跟我去；我可以告诉你为什么他的死是必要的，你听了就会知道这是你的一件无可推辞的行动。现在正是晚餐的时候，夜过去得很快，准备起来吧。

罗德利哥 我还要听一听你要教我这样做的理由。

伊阿古 我一定可以向你解释明白。

同下。

SCENE III

Another room In the castle.

Enter OTHELLO, LODOVICO, DESDEMONA, EMILIA and Attendants.

LODOVICO I do beseech you, sir, trouble yourself no further.

OTHELLO O, pardon me: 'twill do me good to walk.

LODOVICO Madam, good night; I humbly thank your ladyship.

DESDEMONA Your honour is most welcome.

OTHELLO Will you walk, sir?
O,—Desdemona,—

DESDEMONA My lord?

OTHELLO Get you to bed on the instant; I will be returned forthwith: dismiss your attendant there: look it be done.

DESDEMONA I will, my lord.

Exeunt OTHELLO, LODOVICO, and Attendants.

EMILIA How goes it now? he looks gentler than he did.

DESDEMONA He says he will return incontinent:
He hath commanded me to go to bed,
And bade me to dismiss you.

EMILIA Dismiss me!

DESDEMONA It was his bidding: therefore, good Emilia,.
Give me my nightly wearing, and adieu:
We must not now displease him.

EMILIA I would you had never seen him!

DESDEMONA So would not I my love doth so approve him,
That even his stubbornness,his cheques,his frowns—
Prithee, unpin me,—have grace and favour in them.

EMILIA I have laid those sheets you bade me on the bed.

DESDEMONA All's one. Good faith, how foolish are our minds!

第三场

城堡中另一室。

奥瑟罗、罗多维利、苔丝狄蒙娜、爱米利娅及侍从等上。

罗多维科 将军请留步吧。

奥 瑟 罗 啊，没有关系，散散步对我也是很有好处的。

罗多维科 夫人，晚安，谢谢您的盛情。

苔丝狄蒙娜 大驾光临，我们是十分欢迎的。

奥 瑟 罗 请吧，大人。啊！苔丝狄蒙娜——

苔丝狄蒙娜 我的主？

奥 瑟 罗 你快进去睡吧，我马上就回来的。把你的侍女们打发开了，不要忘记。

苔丝狄蒙娜 是，我的主。

奥瑟罗、罗多维科及侍从等下。

爱米利娅 怎么？他现在的脸色温和得多啦。

苔丝狄蒙娜 他说他就会回来的；他叫我去睡，还叫我把你遣开。

爱米利娅 把我遣开！

苔丝狄蒙娜 这是他的吩咐，所以，好爱米利娅，把我的睡衣给我，你去吧，我们现在不能再惹他生气了。

爱米利娅 我希望您当初并不和他相识！

苔丝狄蒙娜 我却不希望这样；我是那么喜欢他，即使他的固执、他的呵斥、他的怒容——请你替我取下衣上的扣针——在我看来也是可爱的。

爱米利娅 我已经照您的吩咐，把那些被褥铺好了。

苔丝狄蒙娜 很好。天哪！我们的思想是多么傻！要是我比你先死，请你就把

If I do die before thee prithee, shroud me
In one of those same sheets.

EMILIA Come, come you talk.

DESDEMONA My mother had a maid call'd Barbara:
She was in love, and he she loved proved mad
And did forsake her: she had a song of 'willow;'
An old thing 'twas, but it express'd her fortune,
And she died singing it: that song to-night
Will not go from my mind; I have much to do,
But to go hang my head all at one side,
And sing it like poor Barbara. Prithee, dispatch.

EMILIA Shall I go fetch your night-gown?

DESDEMONA No, unpin me here.
This Lodovico is a proper man.

EMILIA A very handsome man.

DESDEMONA He speaks well.

EMILIA I know a lady in Venice would have walked barefoot to Palestine for a touch of his nether lip.

DESDEMONA *[Singing]*
The poor soul sat sighing by a sycamore tree,
Sing all a green willow:
Her hand on her bosom, her head on her knee,
Sing willow, willow, willow:
The fresh streams ran by her, and murmur'd her moans;
Sing willow, willow, willow;
Her salt tears fell from her, and soften'd the stones;
Lay by these:—
[Singing]
Sing willow, willow, willow;
Prithee, hie thee; he'll come anon:—
[Singing]
Sing all a green willow must be my garland.

那些被褥做我的殓衾。

爱米利娅 得啦得啦，您在说呆话。

苔丝狄蒙娜 我的母亲有一个侍女名叫巴巴拉，她跟人家有了恋爱；她的情人发了疯，把她丢了。她有一支《杨柳歌》，那是一支古老的曲调，可是正好说中了她的命运；她到死的时候，嘴里还在唱着它。那支歌今天晚上老是萦回在我的脑际；我的烦乱的心绪，使我禁不住侧下我的头，学着可怜的巴巴拉的样子把它歌唱。请你赶快点儿。

爱米利娅 我要不要就去把您的睡衣拿来？

苔丝狄蒙娜 不，先替我取下这儿的扣针。这个罗多维科是一个俊美的男子。

爱米利娅 一个很漂亮的人。

苔丝狄蒙娜 他的谈吐很高雅。

爱米利娅 我知道威尼斯有一个女郎，愿意赤了脚步行到巴勒斯坦，为了希望碰一碰他的下唇。

苔丝狄蒙娜 （唱）

可怜的她坐在枫树下啜泣，
歌唱那青青杨柳；
她手抚着胸膛，她低头靠膝，
唱杨柳，杨柳，杨柳。
清澈的流水吐出她的呻吟，
唱杨柳，杨柳，杨柳。
她的热泪溶化了顽石的心——
把这些放在一旁。——
（唱）
唱杨柳，杨柳，杨柳。
快一点，他就要来了。——
（唱）
青青的柳枝编成一个翠环；

Let nobody blame him; his scorn I approve,-
Nay, that's not next.—Hark! who is't that knocks?

EMILIA It's the wind.

DESDEMONA *[Singing]*
I call'd my love false love; but what said he then?
Sing willow, willow, willow:
If I court moe women, you'll couch with moe men!
So, get thee gone; good night Ate eyes do itch;
Doth that bode weeping?

EMILIA 'Tis neither here nor there.

DESDEMONA I have heard it said so. O, these men, these men!
Dost thou in conscience think,—tell me, Emilia,—
That there be women do abuse their husbands
In such gross kind?

EMILIA There be some such, no question.

DESDEMONA Wouldst thou do such a deed for all the world?

EMILIA Why, would not you?

DESDEMONA No, by this heavenly light!

EMILIA Nor I neither by this heavenly light; I might do't as well i' the dark.

DESDEMONA Wouldst thou do such a deed for all the world?

EMILIA The world's a huge thing: it is a great price
for a small vice.

DESDEMONA In troth, I think thou wouldst not.

EMILIA In troth, I think I should; and undo't when I had done. Marry, I would not do such a thing for a joint-ring, nor for measures of lawn, nor for gowns, petticoats, nor caps, nor any petty exhibition; but for the whole world,—why, who would not make her husband a cuckold to make him a monarch? I should venture purgatory for't.

DESDEMONA Beshrew me, if I would do such a wrong
for the whole world.

不要怪他，我甘心受他笑骂——

不，下面一句不是这样的。听！谁在打门？

爱米利娅 是风哩。

苔丝狄蒙娜 （唱）

我叫情哥负心郎，他又怎讲？

唱杨柳，杨柳，杨柳。

我见异思迁，由你另换情郎。

你去吧，晚安。我的眼睛在跳，那是哭泣的预兆吗？

爱米利娅 没有这样的事。

苔丝狄蒙娜 我听见人家这样说。啊，这些男人！这些男人！凭你的良心说，爱米利娅，你想世上有没有背着丈夫干这种坏事的女人？

爱米利娅 怎么没有？

苔丝狄蒙娜 你愿意为了整个世界的财富而干这种事吗？

爱米利娅 难道您不愿意吗？

苔丝狄蒙娜 不，我对着明月起誓！

爱米利娅 不，对着光天化日，我也不干这种事，要干也得暗地里干。

苔丝狄蒙娜 难道你愿意为了整个的世界而干这种事吗？

爱米利娅 世界是一个大东西；用一件小小的坏事换得这样大的代价是值得的。

苔丝狄蒙娜 真的，我想你不会。

爱米利娅 真的，我想我应该干的。等干好之后，再想法补救。当然，为了一枚对合的戒指、几丈细麻布或是几件衣服、几件裙子、一两顶帽子，以及诸如此类的小玩意儿而叫我干这种事，我当然不愿意。可是为了整个的世界，谁不愿意出卖自己的贞操，让她的丈夫做一个皇帝呢？我就是因此而下炼狱，也是甘心的。

苔丝狄蒙娜 我要是为了整个的世界，会干出这种丧心病狂的事来，一定不得好死。

EMILIA Why the wrong is but a wrong i' the world: and having the world for your labour, tis a wrong in your own world, and you might quickly make it right.

DESDEMONA I do not think there is any such woman.

EMILIA Yes, a dozen; and as many to the vantage as would store the world they played for.

But I do think it is their husbands' faults
If wives do fall: say that they slack their duties,
And pour our treasures into foreign laps,
Or else break out in peevish jealousies,
Throwing restraint upon us; or say they strike us,
Or scant our former having in despite;
Why, we have galls, and though we have some grace,
Yet have we some revenge. Let husbands know
Their wives have sense like them: they see and smell
And have their palates both for sweet and sour,
As husbands have. What is it that they do
When they change us for others? Is it sport?
I think it is: and doth affection breed it?
I think it doth: is't frailty that thus errs?
It is so too: and have not we affections,
Desires for sport, and frailty, as men have?
Then let them use us well: else let them know,
The ills we do, their ills instruct us so.

DESDEMONA

Good night, good night: heaven me such uses send,
Not to pick bad from bad, but by bad mend!

Exeunt.

爱米利娅 世间的是非本来没有定准；您因为干了一件错事而得到整个的世界，在您自己的世界里，您还不能把是非颠倒过来吗？

苔丝狄蒙娜 我想世上不会有那样的女人的。

爱米利娅 这样的女人不是几个，可多着呢，足够把她们用小小的坏事换来的世界塞满了。照我想来，妻子的堕落总是丈夫的过失；要是他们疏忽了自己的责任，把我们所珍爱的东西浪掷在外人的怀里，或是无缘无故吃起醋来，约束我们行动的自由，或是殴打我们，削减我们的花粉钱，我们也是有脾气的，虽然生就温柔的天性，到了一个时候也是会复仇的。让做丈夫的人们知道，他们的妻子也和他们有同样的感觉：她们的眼睛也能辨别美恶，她们的鼻子也能辨别香臭，她们的舌头也能辨别甜酸，正像她们的丈夫们一样。他们厌弃了我们，别寻新欢，是为了什么缘故呢？是逢场作戏吗？我想是的。是因为爱情的驱使吗？我想也是的。还是因为喜新厌旧的人之常情呢？那也是一个理由。那么难道我们就不会对别人发生爱情，难道我们就没有逢场作戏的欲望，难道我们就不会喜新厌旧，跟男人们一样吗？所以让他们好好地对待我们吧；否则我们要让他们知道，我们所干的坏事都是出于他们的指教。

苔丝狄蒙娜 晚安，晚安！愿上天监视我们的言行；我不愿以恶为师，我只愿鉴非自警！

各下。

ACT V 第五幕

SCENE I

Cyprus. A street.
Enter IAGO and RODERIGO.

IAGO Here, stand behind this bulk; straight will he come:
Wear thy good rapier bare, and put it home:
Quick, quick; fear nothing; I'll be at thy elbow:
It makes us, or it mars us; think on that,
And fix most firm thy resolution.

RODERIGO Be near at hand; I may miscarry in't.

IAGO Here, at thy hand: be bold, and take thy stand.

Retires.

RODERIGO I have no great devotion to the deed;
And yet he hath given me satisfying reasons:
'Tis but a man gone. Forth, my sword: he dies.

IAGO I have rubb'd this young quat almost to the sense,
And he grows angry. Now, whether he kill Cassio,
Or Cassio him, or each do kill the other,
Every way makes my gain: live Roderigo,
He calls me to a restitution large
Of gold and jewels that I bobb'd from him,
As gifts to Desdemona;
It must not be: if Cassio do remain,
He hath a daily beauty in his life
That makes me ugly; and, besides, the Moor
May unfold me to him; there stand I in much peril:
No, he must die. But so: I hear him coming.

Enter CASSIO.

RODERIGO I know his gait, 'tis he.—Villain, thou diest!

第一场

塞浦路斯。街道。
伊阿古及罗德利哥上。

伊阿古　来，站在这堵披屋后面。他就会来的。把你的宝剑拔出鞘来，看准要害刺过去。快，快，不要怕，我就在你旁边。成功失败，在此一举，你得下定决心。

罗德利哥　不要走开，也许我会失手。

伊阿古　我就在这儿，你的近旁。胆子放大些，站定了。

退后。

罗德利哥　我对于这件事情不是顶热心，可是他讲的理由十分充足。反正不过去掉一个人。出来，我的剑，他必须死！

伊阿古　我已经激动这小脓包的心，他居然动起怒来了。不管是他杀死凯西奥，还是凯西奥杀死他，或者两败俱伤，对于我都是有好处的。要是罗德利哥活在世上，他总有一天要问我讨还那许多我从他手里吞没下来、说是送给苔丝狄蒙娜的金银珠宝；这可断断不能。要是凯西奥活在世上，他那种翩翩风度，叫我每天都要在他的旁边相形见绌；而且那摩尔人万一向他当面质问起来，我的阴谋就会暴露，那时候我的地位就非常危险了。不，他非死不可。就这样吧。我听见他来了。

凯西奥上。

罗德利哥　我认识他的走路的姿势，正是他。——恶人，你给我死吧！

Makes a pass at CASSIO.

CASSIO That thrust had been mine enemy indeed,
But that my coat is better than thou know'st
I will make proof of thine.

Draws, and wounds RODERIGO.

RODERIGO O, I am slain!

IAGO from behind wounds CASSIO in the leg, and exit.

CASSIO I am maim'd for ever. Help, ho! murder! murder!

Falls.
Enter OTHELLO.

OTHELLO The voice of Cassio: Iago keeps his word.

RODERIGO O, villain that I am!

OTHELLO It is even so.

CASSIO O, help, ho! light! a surgeon!

OTHELLO 'Tis he:—O brave Iago, honest and just,
That hast such noble sense of thy friend's wrong!
Thou teachest me. Minion, your dear lies dead,
And your unblest fate hies: strumpet, I come.
Forth of my heart those charms, thine eyes, are blotted;
Thy bed, lust-stain'd, shall with lust's blood be spotted.

Exit.
Enter LODOVICO and GRATIANO.

CASSIO What, ho! no watch? no passage? murder! murder!

GRATIANO 'Tis some mischance; the cry is very direful.

CASSIO O, help!

挺剑刺凯西奥。

凯 西 奥　幸亏我穿着一身好甲，否则那一剑一定会致我的死命。让我也来试一试你的甲牢不牢吧。

拔剑刺伤罗德利哥。

罗德利哥　啊，我死了！

伊阿古自后刺伤凯西奥腿，下。

凯 西 奥　我从此终身残废了！救命啊！杀了人啦！杀了人啦！

倒地。
奥瑟罗自远处上。

奥 瑟 罗　凯西奥的声音。伊阿古果然没有失信。

罗德利哥　啊，我真是个恶人！

奥 瑟 罗　一点不错。

凯 西 奥　啊，救命哪！拿火来！找一个医生！

奥 瑟 罗　正是他。勇敢正直的伊阿古呀，你这样奋不顾身，为你的朋友复仇雪耻，真是难得！你给我一个教训了。贱人，你心爱的人已经死在这儿，你的末日就在眼前。娼妇，我来了！从我的心头抹去你的媚眼的魔力；让淫邪的血溅洒你那被淫邪玷污了的枕席。

下。
罗多维科及葛莱西安诺自远处上。

凯 西 奥　喂！怎么！没有巡夜的逻卒？没有过路的行人？杀了人啦！杀了人啦！

葛莱西安诺　出了什么乱子啦？这叫声很是凄惨。

凯 西 奥　救命啊！

LODOVICO Hark!

RODERIGO O wretched villain!

LODOVICO Two or three groan: it is a heavy night:
These may be counterfeits: let's think't unsafe
To come in to the cry without more help.

RODERIGO Nobody come? then shall I bleed to death.

LODOVICO Hark!

Re-enter IAGO, with a light.

GRATIANO Here's one comes in his shirt, with light and weapons.

IAGO Who's there? whose noise is this that ones on murder?

LODOVICO We do not know.

IAGO Did not you hear a cry?

CASSIO Here, here! for heaven's sake, help me!

IAGO What's the matter?

GRATIANO This is Othello's ancient, as I take it.

LODOVICO The same indeed; a very valiant fellow.

IAGO What are you here that cry so grievously?

CASSIO Iago? O, I am spoil'd, undone by villains!
Give me some help.

IAGO O me, lieutenant! what villains have done this?

CASSIO I think that one of them is hereabout,
And cannot make away.

IAGO O treacherous villains!
What are you there? come in, and give some help.

To LODOVICO and GRATIANO.

RODERIGO O, help me here!

CASSIO That's one of them.

IAGO O murderous slave! O villain!

Stabs RODERIGO.

罗多维科　听！

罗德利哥　啊，该死的恶人！

罗多维科　两三个人在那儿呻吟。这是一个很阴沉的黑夜；也许他们是故意假装出来的，我们人手孤单，冒冒失失过去，恐怕不大安全。

罗德利哥　没有人来吗？那么我要流血而死了！

罗多维科　听！

伊阿古持火炬重上。

葛莱西安诺　有一个人穿着衬衫、一手拿火、一手举着武器来了。

伊 阿 古　那边是谁？什么人在那儿喊杀人？

罗多维科　我们不知道。

伊 阿 古　你们听见一个呼声吗？

凯 西 奥　这儿，这儿！看在上天的面上，救救我！

伊 阿 古　怎么一回事？

葛莱西安诺　这个人好像是奥瑟罗麾下的旗官。

罗多维科　正是，一个很勇敢的汉子。

伊 阿 古　你是什么人，在这儿叫喊得这样凄惨？

凯 西 奥　伊阿古吗？啊，我被恶人算计，害得我不能做人啦！救救我！

伊 阿 古　嗳哟，副将！这是什么恶人干的事？

凯 西 奥　我想有一个暴徒还在这儿，他逃不了。

伊 阿 古　啊，可恶的奸贼！你们是什么人？过来帮帮忙。

向罗多维科、葛莱西安诺。

罗德利哥　啊，救救我！我在这儿。

凯 西 奥　他就是恶党中的一人。

伊 阿 古　好一个杀人的凶徒！啊，恶人！

刺罗德利哥。

RODERIGO O damn'd Iago! O inhuman dog!

IAGO Kill men i' the dark!—
Where be these bloody thieves?—
How silent is this town!—Ho! murder! murder!—
What may you be? are you of good or evil?

LODOVICO As you shall prove us, praise us.

IAGO Signior Lodovico?

LODOVICO He, sir.

IAGO I cry you mercy. Here's Cassio hurt by villains.

GRATIANO Cassio!

IAGO How is't, brother!

CASSIO My leg is cut in two.

IAGO Marry, heaven forbid!
Light, gentlemen; I'll bind it with my shirt.

Enter BIANCA.

BIANCA What is the matter, ho? who is't that cried?

IAGO Who is't that cried!

BIANCA O my dear Cassio! my sweet Cassio! O Cassio,
Cassio, Cassio!

IAGO O notable strumpet! Cassio, may you suspect
Who they should be that have thus many led you?

CASSIO No.

GRATIANO I am to find you thus: I have been to seek you.

IAGO Lend me a garter. So. O, for a chair,
To bear him easily hence!

BIANCA Alas, he faints! O Cassio, Cassio, Cassio!

IAGO Gentlemen all, I do suspect this trash
To be a party in this injury.
Patience awhile, good Cassio. Come, come;
Lend me a light. Know we this face or no?

罗德利哥 啊，万恶的伊阿古！没有人心的狗！

伊 阿 古 在暗地里杀人！这些凶恶的贼党都在哪儿？这地方多么寂静！喂！杀了人啦！杀了人啦！你们是什么人？是好人还是坏人？

罗多维科 请你自己判断我们吧。

伊 阿 古 罗多维科大人吗？

罗多维科 正是，老总。

伊 阿 古 恕我失礼了。这儿是凯西奥，被恶人们刺伤，倒在地上。

葛莱西安诺 凯西奥！

伊 阿 古 怎么样，兄弟？

凯 西 奥 我的腿断了。

伊 阿 古 嗳哟，罪过罪过！两位先生，请替我照着亮儿；我要用我的衫子把它包扎起来。

比恩卡上。

比 恩 卡 喂，什么事？谁在这儿叫喊？

伊 阿 古 谁在这儿叫喊！

比 恩 卡 嗳哟，我的亲爱的凯西奥！我的温柔的凯西奥！啊，凯西奥！凯西奥！凯西奥！

伊 阿 古 哼，你这声名狼藉的娼妇！凯西奥，照你猜想起来，向你下这样毒手的大概是些什么人？

凯 西 奥 我不知道。

葛莱西安诺 我正要来找你，谁料你会遭逢这样的祸事，真是恼人！

伊 阿 古 借给我一条吊袜带。好。啊，要是有一张椅子，让他舒舒服服躺在上面，把他抬去才好！

比 恩 卡 嗳哟，他晕过去了！啊，凯西奥！凯西奥！凯西奥！

伊 阿 古 两位先生，我很疑心这个贱人也是那些凶徒们的同党。——忍耐点儿，好凯西奥。——来，来，借我一个火。我们认不认识这一张面孔？嗳哟！是我的同国好友罗德利哥吗？不。唉，果然是他！天哪！罗德利哥！

Alas my friend and my dear countryman
Roderigo! no:—yes, sure: O heaven! Roderigo.

GRATIANO What, of Venice?

IAGO Even he, sir; did you know him?

GRATIANO Know him! ay.

IAGO Signior Gratiano? I cry you gentle pardon;
These bloody accidents must excuse my manners,
That so neglected you.

GRATIANO I am glad to see you.

IAGO How do you, Cassio? O, a chair, a chair!

GRATIANO Roderigo!

IAGO He, he 'tis he.
[A chair brought in]
O, that's well said; the chair!
Some good man bear him carefully from hence;
I'll fetch the general's surgeon.
[To BIANCA] For you, mistress,
Save you your labour. He that lies slain here, Cassio,
Was my dear friend: what malice was between you?

CASSIO None in the world; nor do I know the man.

IAGO *[To BIANCA]* What, look you pale? O, bear him out o' the air.

CASSIO and RODERIGO are borne off.

Stay you, good gentlemen. Look you pale, mistress?
Do you perceive the gastness of her eye?
Nay, if you stare, we shall hear more anon.
Behold her well; I pray you, look upon her:
Do you see, gentlemen? nay, guiltiness will speak,
Though tongues were out of use.

Enter EMILIA.

葛莱西安诺　什么！威尼斯的罗德利哥吗？

伊阿古　正是他，先生。你认识他吗？

葛莱西安诺　认识他！我怎么不认识他？

伊阿古　葛莱西安诺先生吗？请您原谅，这些流血的惨剧，使我礼貌不周，失敬得很。

葛莱西安诺　哪儿的话,我很高兴看见您。

伊阿古　你怎么啦，凯西奥？啊，来一张椅子！来一张椅子！

葛莱西安诺　罗德利哥！

伊阿古　他，他，正是他。（众人携椅上）啊！很好，椅子。几个人把他小心抬走；我就去找军医官来。（向比恩卡）你，奶奶，你也不用装腔作势啦。——凯西奥，死在这儿的这个人是我的好朋友。你们两人有什么仇恨？

凯西奥　一点没有,我根本不认识这个人。

伊阿古　（向比恩卡）什么！你脸色变白了吗？——啊！把他抬进屋子里去。

众人舁凯西奥、罗德利哥二人下。

等一等，两位先生。奶奶，你脸色变白了吗？你们看见她眼睛里这一股惊慌的神气吗？哼，要是你这样睁大了眼睛，我们还要等着听一些新鲜的话哩。留心瞧着她；你们瞧；你们看见了吗，两位先生？哼，犯了罪的人，即使舌头僵住了，也会不打自招的。

爱米利娅上。

EMILIA 'Las, what's the matter? what's the matter, husband?

IAGO Cassio hath here been set on in the dark
By Roderigo and fellows that are'scap'd:
He's almost slain, and Roderigo dead.

EMILIA Alas, good gentleman! alas, good Cassio!

IAGO This is the fruit of whoring. Prithee, Emilia,
Go know of Cassio where he supp'd to-night.

To BIANCA.

What, do you shake at that?

BIANCA He supp'd at my house; but I therefore shake not.

IAGO O, did he so? I charge you, go with me.

EMILIA Fie, fie upon thee, strumpet!

BIANCA I am no strumpet; but of life as honest
As you that thus abuse me.

EMILIA As I! foh! fie upon thee!

IAGO Kind gentlemen, let's go see poor Cassio dress'd.
Come, mistress, you must tell's another tale.
Emilia run you to the citadel,
And tell my lord and lady what hath happ'd.
Will you go on? I pray.
[Aside] This is the night
That either makes me or fordoes me quite.

Exeunt.

爱米利娅 唉！出了什么事啦？出了什么事啦，丈夫？

伊 阿 古 凯西奥在这儿黑暗之中，被罗德利哥和几个在逃的同党袭击；他几乎送了性命，罗德利哥已经死了。

爱米利娅 嗳哟，好一位绅士！嗳哟，好凯西奥！

伊 阿 古 这是他爱嫖的结果。爱米利娅，你去问问凯西奥，他今天晚上在什么地方吃饭的。

向比恩卡。

——什么！你听了这句话就发抖吗？

比 恩 卡 他在我家里吃饭，可我并不是因为这个而发抖。

伊 阿 古 噢，他在你家里吃饭？你跟我走！

爱米利娅 呸，呸，你这不要脸的娼妇！

比 恩 卡 我不是娼妇，我跟你一样清白。

爱米利娅 跟我一样清白！呸！不要脸！

伊 阿 古 两位好先生，让我们去帮助帮助可怜的凯西奥，替他把伤口扎好。来，奶奶，你必须对我们讲老实话。爱米利娅，你快奔到城堡里去，告诉将军和夫人这儿发生了什么事。你们先请吧。（旁白）今夜是我的命运所寄，倘不能青云直上，就要一败涂地。

同下。

SCENE Ⅱ

A bedchamber in the castle:
Enter OTHELLODESDEMONA in bed asleep;a light burning.

OTHELLO It is the cause, it is the cause, my soul,—
Let me not name it to you, you chaste stars!—
It is the cause. Yet I'll not shed her blood;
Nor scar that whiter skin of hers than snow,
And smooth as monumental alabaster.
Yet she must die, else she'll betray more men.
Put out the light, and then put out the light:
If I quench thee, thou flaming minister,
I can again thy former light restore,
Should I repent me: but once put out thy light,
Thou cunning'st pattern of excelling nature,
I know not where is that Promethean heat
That can thy light relume. When I have pluck'd the rose,
I cannot give it vital growth again.
It must needs wither: I'll smell it on the tree.
[Kissing her]
Ah balmy breath, that dost almost persuade
Justice to break her sword! One more, one more.
Be thus when thou art dead, and I will kill thee,
And love thee after. One more, and this the last:
So sweet was ne'er so fatal. I must weep,
But they are cruel tears: this sorrow's heavenly;
It strikes where it doth love. She wakes.

DESDEMONA Who's there? Othello?

OTHELLO Ay. Desdemona.

DESDEMONA Will you come to bed, my lord?

OTHELLO Have you pray'd to-night, Desdemona?

第二场

城堡中的卧室。

苔丝狄蒙娜睡床上，一灯照耀室内；奥瑟罗上。

奥瑟罗 只是为了这一个原因，只是为了这一个原因，我的灵魂！纯洁的星星啊，不要让我向你们说出它的名字！只是为了这一个原因……可是我不愿溅她的血，也不愿毁伤她那比白雪更皎洁、比石膏更腻滑的肌肤。可是她不能不死，否则她将要陷害更多的男子。让我熄灭了这一盏灯，然后我就熄灭你的生命的火焰。融融的灯光啊，我把你吹熄以后，要是我心生后悔，仍旧可以把你重新点亮。可是你，造化最精美的形象啊，你的火焰一旦熄灭，我不知道什么地方有那天上的神火，能够燃起你的原来的光彩！我摘下了蔷薇，就不能再给它已失的生机，只好让它枯萎凋谢；当它还在枝头的时候，我要嗅一嗅它的芳香。（吻苔丝狄蒙娜）啊，甘美的气息！你几乎诱动公道的心，使她折断她的利剑了！再一个吻，再一个吻。愿你到死都是这样；我要杀死你，然后再爱你。再一个吻，这是最后的一吻了；这样销魂，却又是这样无比的惨痛！我必须哭泣，然而这些是无情的眼泪。这一阵阵悲伤是神圣的，因为它要惩罚的正是它最疼爱的。她醒来了。

苔丝狄蒙娜 谁？奥瑟罗吗？

奥瑟罗 嗯，苔丝狄蒙娜。

苔丝狄蒙娜 您要睡了吗，我的主？

奥瑟罗 你今晚有没有祈祷过，苔丝狄蒙娜？

DESDEMONA Ay, my lord.

OTHELLO If you bethink yourself of any crime
Unreconciled as yet to heaven and grace,
Solicit for it straight.

DESDEMONA Alas, my lord, what do you mean by that?

OTHELLO Well, do it, and be brief; I will walk by:
I would not kill thy unprepared spirit;
No; heaven forfend! I would not kill thy soul.

DESDEMONA Talk you of killing?

OTHELLO Ay, I do.

DESDEMONA Then heaven
Have mercy on me!

OTHELLO Amen, with all my heart!

DESDEMONA If you say so, I hope you will not kill me.

OTHELLO Hum!

DESDEMONA And yet I fear you; for you are fatal then
When your eyes roll so: why I should fear I know not,
Since guiltiness I know not; but yet I feel I fear.

OTHELLO Think on thy sins.

DESDEMONA They are loves I bear to you.

OTHELLO Ay, and for that thou diest.

DESDEMONA That death's unnatural that kills for loving.
Alas, why gnaw you so your nether lip?
Some bloody passion shakes your very frame:
These are portents; but yet I hope, I hope,
They do not point on me.

OTHELLO Peace, and be still!

DESDEMONA I will so. What's the matter?

OTHELLO That handkerchief which I so lov'd and gave thee
Thou gav'st to Cassio.

DESDEMONA No, by my life and soul!
Send for the man, and ask him.

苔丝狄蒙娜 祈祷过了，我的主。

奥瑟罗 要是你想到在你的一生之中，还有什么罪恶不曾为上帝所宽宥，赶快恳求他的恩赦吧。

苔丝狄蒙娜 嗳哟！我的主，您这句话是什么意思？

奥瑟罗 嘿，祈祷吧，干脆点儿，我就在一旁等着你。我不愿杀害你的没有准备的灵魂；不，上天禁止这种罪行！我不愿杀害你的灵魂。

苔丝狄蒙娜 您在说杀人的话吗？

奥瑟罗 嗯，是的。

苔丝狄蒙娜 那么愿上天垂怜于我！

奥瑟罗 阿门，但愿如此！

苔丝狄蒙娜 要是您这样说，我希望您不至于把我杀死。

奥瑟罗 哼！

苔丝狄蒙娜 可是我怕您，因为您的眼珠这样滚转的时候，您已经动了杀机。我不知道我为什么害怕，因为我不知道我有什么罪，可是我觉得害怕。

奥瑟罗 想想你的罪恶吧。

苔丝狄蒙娜 除非我对您的爱是罪恶，我不知道我有什么罪恶。

奥瑟罗 好，你必须因此而死。

苔丝狄蒙娜 为了爱而被杀，那样的死是违反人情的。唉！您为什么这样咬着您的下唇呢？一种饮血的欲念震撼您的全身，这便是它的征兆。可是我希望，我希望您的怒气不是对我而发。

奥瑟罗 闭嘴，不要作声！

苔丝狄蒙娜 是。可是请您告诉我究竟为了什么事？

奥瑟罗 你把我给你的那条我的心爱的手帕送给凯西奥。

苔丝狄蒙娜 不，凭着我的生命和灵魂起誓！您叫他来问好了。

OTHELLO Sweet soul, take heed, Take heed of perjury; thou art on thy deathbed.

DESDEMONA Ay, but not yet to die.

OTHELLO Yes, presently:
Therefore confess thee freely of thy sin;
For to deny each article with oath
Cannot remove nor choke the strong conception
That I do groan withal. Thou art to die.

DESDEMONA Then Lord have mercy on me!

OTHELLO I say, amen.

DESDEMONA And have you mercy too! I never did
Offend you in my life; never loved Cassio
But with such general warranty of heaven
As I might love: I never gave him token.

OTHELLO By heaven, I saw my handkerchief in's hand.
O perjured woman! thou dost stone my heart,
And mak'st me call what I intend to do
A murder, which I thought a sacrifice:
I saw the handkerchief.

DESDEMONA He found it then;
I never gave it him: send for him hither;
Let him confess a truth.

OTHELLO He hath confess'd.

DESDEMONA What, my lord?

OTHELLO That he hath used thee.

DESDEMONA How? unlawfully?

OTHELLO Ay.

DESDEMONA He will not say so.

OTHELLO No, his mouth is stopp'd;
Honest Iago hath ta'en order for't.

DESDEMONA O! my fear interprets: what, is he dead?

OTHELLO Had all his hairs been lives, my great revenge

奥瑟罗 好人儿，留心不要发伪誓，你的死已在眼前了。

苔丝狄蒙娜 不，我现在还不能死。

奥瑟罗 你必须立刻死，所以赶快坦白招认你的罪恶吧；即使你发誓否认每一件事实，也不能除去那使我痛心的坚强的确信。你必须死。

苔丝狄蒙娜 那么愿上帝垂怜于我！

奥瑟罗 阿门。

苔丝狄蒙娜 愿您也大发慈悲！我生平从不曾得罪过您，也从不曾用上天所不容的非分的爱情滥施在凯西奥的身上；我没有给过他什么东西。

奥瑟罗 苍天在上，我亲眼看见我的手帕在他的手里。欺罔神明的妇人！你使我的心变成坚硬；我本来想把你作为献祭的牺牲，现在却被你激起我的屠夫的恶念来了。我明明看见那手帕的。

苔丝狄蒙娜 那么他是在什么地方拾到的，我没有给他。叫他到这儿来，让他供认事实的真相。

奥瑟罗 他已经承认了。

苔丝狄蒙娜 承认什么，我的主？

奥瑟罗 承认他已经和你发生关系。

苔丝狄蒙娜 怎么？非法的关系吗？

奥瑟罗 嗯。

苔丝狄蒙娜 他不会这样说的。

奥瑟罗 是的，他的嘴已经闭住，正直的伊阿古已经把他解决了。

苔丝狄蒙娜 啊，我的恐惧叫我明白过来了！什么！他死了吗？

奥瑟罗 即使他每一根头发里都有生命，我的复仇的怒火也会把它们一起

Had stomach for them all.

DESDEMONA Alas! he is betray'd and I undone.

OTHELLO Out, strumpet! weep'st thou for him to my face?

DESDEMONA O, banish me, my lord, but kill me not!

OTHELLO Down, strumpet!

DESDEMONA Kill me tomorrow: let me live to-night!

OTHELLO Nay, if you strive—

DESDEMONA But half an hour!

OTHELLO Being done, there is no pause.

DESDEMONA But while I say one prayer!

OTHELLO It is too late.

He stifles her.

EMILIA *[Within]* My lord , my lord! what, ho! my lord, my lord!

OTHELLO What noise is this? Not dead? not yet quite dead?
I that am cruel am yet merciful;
I would not have thee linger in thy pain: So, so.

Stab DESDEMONA.

EMILIA *[Within]* What, ho! my lord, my lord!

OTHELLO Who's there?

EMILIA *[Within]* O, good my lord, I would speak a word with you!

OTHELLO Yes: 'tis Emilia. By and by. She's dead.
'Tis like she comes to speak of Cassio's death.—
The noise was here. Ha! no more moving?
Still as the grave.
Shall she come in? were't good?—
I think she stirs again:—no. What's best to do?
If she come in, she'll sure speak to my wife:
My wife! my wife! what wife? I have no wife.
O insupportable! O heavy hour!

吞下。

苔丝狄蒙娜 唉！他被人陷害，我的一生也从此断送了！

奥瑟罗 不要脸的娼妇！你当着我的面为他哭泣吗？

苔丝狄蒙娜 啊，我的主，把我放逐，可是不要杀我！

奥瑟罗 倒下，娼妇！

苔丝狄蒙娜 明天杀我，让我活过今天！

奥瑟罗 不，要是你想挣扎——

苔丝狄蒙娜 给我半点钟的时间！

奥瑟罗 已经决定了，没有挽回的余地。

苔丝狄蒙娜 可是让我作一次祷告吧！

奥瑟罗 太迟了。

扼苔丝狄蒙娜咽喉。

爱米利娅 （在内）将军，将军！喂！将军，将军！

奥瑟罗 这是什么声音？没有死吗？还没有完全死去吗？我虽然狠心，却还有几分慈悲；我不愿你多挨受一刻痛苦。好，好。

刺苔丝狄蒙娜。

爱米利娅 （在内）喂！将军，将军！

奥瑟罗 哪一个？

爱米利娅 （在内）啊，将军！我要跟您说句话儿。

奥瑟罗 是的，这是爱米利娅。——等一等。——她死了。她多半要来说起凯西奥的死。外边已经听得见嘈杂的声音。嘿！一动也不动了吗？像坟墓一样沉寂。要不要让她进来？妥当不妥当？我想她又在动了，不，怎么办呢？要是她进来，她一定要跟我的妻子说话。我的妻子！我的妻子！什么妻子？我没有妻子。啊，难堪！啊，不幸的时辰！我想现在日月应该晦暗不明，受惊的地球看见这种非常的灾变，也要吓得目瞪口呆。

Methinks it should be now a huge eclipse
Of sun and moon, and that the affrighted globe
Should yawn at alteration.

EMILIA *[Within]* I do beseech you
That I may speak with you, O, good my lord!

OTHELLO I had forgot thee: O, come in, Emilia;
Soft; by and by. Let me the curtains draw.
Where art thou?

Unlocks the door.
Enter EMILIA.

OTHELLO What's the matter with thee now?

EMILIA O, my good lord, yonder's foul murders done!

OTHELLO What, now?

EMILIA But now, my lord.

OTHELLO It is the very error of the moon;
She comes more nearer earth than she was wont,
And makes men mad.

EMILIA Cassio, my lord, hath kill'd a young Venetian
Call'd Roderigo.

OTHELLO Roderigo kill'd!
And Cassio kill'd!

EMILIA No, Cassio is not kill'd.

OTHELLO Not Cassio kill'd! then murder's out of tune,
And sweet revenge grows harsh.

DESDEMONA O, falsely, falsely murder'd!

EMILIA Alas, what cry is that?

OTHELLO That! what?

EMILIA Out, and alas! that was my lady's voice.
Help! help, ho! help! O lady, speak again!
Sweet Desdemona! O sweet mistress, speak!

爱米利娅　（在内）啊，好将军！请您让我进来对您说句话儿。

奥 瑟 罗　我忘记了。啊，进来，爱米利娅。慢点儿，等一等。让我把帐幕拉下来。你在哪儿？

启锁开门。
爱米利娅上。

奥 瑟 罗　什么事？
爱米利娅　啊，好将军！那边出了杀人命案啦！
奥 瑟 罗　什么！现在？
爱米利娅　就是刚才，将军。
奥 瑟 罗　那都是因为月亮走错了轨道，比平常更近地球，所以人们都发起疯来了。

爱米利娅　将军，凯西奥杀死了一个名叫罗德利哥的威尼斯青年。

奥 瑟 罗　罗德利哥被杀了！凯西奥也被杀了吗？

爱米利娅　不，凯西奥没有死。
奥 瑟 罗　凯西奥没有死！那么杀人认错了对象，痛快的复仇又有了变卦啦。
苔丝狄蒙娜　啊，死得好冤枉呀！
爱米利娅　嗳哟！那是什么呼声？
奥 瑟 罗　那！什么？
爱米利娅　嗳哟！那是夫人的声音。救命！救命啊！救命！啊，夫人，再说一声话儿！亲爱的苔丝狄蒙娜！啊，亲爱的夫人，说呀！

DESDEMONA A guiltless death I die.
EMILIA O, who hath done this deed?
DESDEMONA Nobody; I myself. Farewell
Commend me to my kind lord: O, farewell!

Dies.

OTHELLO Why, how should she be murder'd?
EMILIA Alas, who knows?
OTHELLO You heard her say herself, it was not I.
EMILIA She said so: I must needs report the truth.
OTHELLO She's, like a liar, gone to burning hell:
'Twas I that kill'd her.
EMILIA O, the more angel she,
And you the blacker devil!
OTHELLO She turn'd to folly, and she was a whore.
EMILIA Thou dost belie her, and thou art a devil.
OTHELLO She was false as water.
EMILIA Thou art rash as fire, to say
That she was false: O, she was heavenly true!
OTHELLO Cassio did top her; ask thy husband else.
O, I were damn'd beneath all depth in hell,
But that I did proceed upon just grounds
To this extremity. Thy husband knew it all.
EMILIA My husband!
OTHELLO Thy husband.
EMILIA That she was false to wedlock?
OTHELLO Ay, with Cassio. Nay, had she been true,
If heaven would make me such another world
Of one entire and Perfect chrysolite,
I'ld not have sold her for it.
EMILIA My husband!
OTHELLO Ay, 'twas he that told me first:

苔丝狄蒙娜 我是无罪而死的。

爱米利娅 啊！这是谁干的事？

苔丝狄蒙娜 谁也没有干，是我自己。再会吧，替我向我的仁慈的夫君致意。啊，再会吧！

死。

奥瑟罗 啊！她怎么会被人杀死的？

爱米利娅 唉！谁知道？

奥瑟罗 你听见她说是她自己，我没有杀死她。

爱米利娅 她是这样说，我只好按照事实去报告。

奥瑟罗 她到地狱的火焰里去，还不愿说一句真话。杀死她的是我。

爱米利娅 啊，那么她尤其是一个天使，你尤其是一个黑心的魔鬼了！

奥瑟罗 她干了无耻的事，她是个淫妇。

爱米利娅 你冤枉她，你是个魔鬼。

奥瑟罗 她像水一样轻浮。

爱米利娅 你说她轻浮，你自己才像火一样粗暴。啊，她是圣洁而忠贞的！

奥瑟罗 凯西奥和她通奸，不信你去问你的丈夫吧。啊，要是我采取这种极端的手段，并没有正当的理由，死后就要永远堕入地狱的底层！你的丈夫一切全都知道。

爱米利娅 我的丈夫！

奥瑟罗 你的丈夫。

爱米利娅 他知道她不守贞节吗？

奥瑟罗 喂，他知道她跟凯西奥有暧昧。嘿，要是她是个贞洁的妇人，即使上帝为我用一颗完整的宝石另外造一个世界，我也不愿用她去交换。

爱米利娅 我的丈夫！

奥瑟罗 嗯，他最初告诉我这件事。他是个正人君子，他痛恨卑鄙龌龊的

An honest man he is, and hates the slime
That sticks on filthy deeds.

EMILIA My husband!

OTHELLO What needs this iteration, woman? I say thy husband.

EMILIA O mistress, villany hath made mocks with love,
My husband say that she was false!

OTHELLO He, woman;
I say thy husband: dost understand the word?
My friend, thy husband, honest, honest Iago.

EMILIA If he say so, may his pernicious soul
Rot half a grain a day! he lies to the heart:
She was too fond of her most filthy bargain.

OTHELLO Ha!

EMILIA Do thy worst:
This deed of thine is no more worthy heaven
Than thou wast worthy her.

OTHELLO Peace, you were best.

EMILIA Thou hast not half that power to do me harm
As I have to be hurt. O gull! O dolt!
As ignorant as dirt! thou hast done a deed—
I care not for thy sword; I'll make thee known,
Though I lost twenty lives.—Help! help, ho! help!
The Moor hath kill'd my mistress! Murder! murder!

Enter MONTANO, GRATIANO, IAGO, and others.

MONTANO What is the matter? How now, general!

EMILIA O, are you come, Iago? you have done well,
That men must lay their murders on your neck.

GRATIANO What is the matter?

EMILIA Disprove this villain, if thou be'st a man:
He says thou told'st him that his wife was false:
I know thou didst not, thou'rt not such a villain:

行为。

爱米利娅 我的丈夫！

奥瑟罗 妇人，为什么把这句话说了又说呢？我是说你的丈夫。

爱米利娅 啊，夫人！你因为多情，受了奸人的愚弄了！我的丈夫说她不贞！

奥瑟罗 正是他，妇人，我说你的丈夫；你懂得这句话吗？我的朋友，你的丈夫，正直的、正直的伊阿古。

爱米利娅 要是他果然说了这样的话，愿他恶毒的灵魂每天一分一寸地糜烂！他全然胡说；她对于她的最卑鄙的男人是太痴心了。

奥瑟罗 嘿！

爱米利娅 随你把我怎么样吧。你配不上这样的好妻子，你这种行为是上天所不容的。

奥瑟罗 还不闭嘴！

爱米利娅 你没有半分力量可以伤害我，我的心碎了，还怕你什么！啊，笨伯！傻瓜！泥土一样蠢的家伙！你已经做了一件大大不该的事——我不怕你的剑；我要宣布你的罪恶，即使我将要因此而丧失二十条生命。救命！救命啊！救命！
摩尔人杀死了夫人啦！杀了人啦！杀了人啦！

蒙太诺、葛莱西安诺、伊阿古及余人等上。

蒙太诺 什么事？怎么，将军！

爱米利娅 啊！你来了吗，伊阿古？你做得好事，人家都把杀人的罪名架在你头上啦！

葛莱西安诺 什么事？

爱米利娅 你倘是个汉子，赶快否认这恶人所说的话吧；他说你告诉他他的妻子不贞。我知道你不会说这种话，你还不会是这样一个恶人。说吧，我的心都要胀破了。

Speak, for my heart is full.

IAGO I told him what I thought, and told no more
Than what he found himself was apt and true.

EMILIA But did you ever tell him she was false?

IAGO I did.

EMILIA You told a lie, an odious, damned lie;
Upon my soul, a lie, a wicked lie.
She false with Cassio!—did you say with Cassio?

IAGO With Cassio, mistress. Go to, charm your tongue.

EMILIA I will not charm my tongue; I am bound to speak:
My mistress here lies murder'd in her bed,—

All O heavens forfend!

EMILIA And your reports have set the murder on.

OTHELLO Nay, stare not, masters: it is true, indeed.

GRATIANO 'Tis a strange truth.

MONTANO O monstrous act!

EMILIA Villany, villany, villany!
I think upon't, I think: I smell't: O villany!—
I thought so then:—I'll kill myself for grief:—
O villany, villany!

IAGO What, are you mad? I charge you, get you home.

EMILIA Good gentlemen, let me have leave to speak:
'Tis proper I obey him, but not now.
Perchance, Iago, I will ne'er go home.

OTHELLO O! O! O!

He falls on the bed.

EMILIA Nay, lay thee down and roar;
For thou hast kill'd the sweetest innocent
That e'er did lift up eye.

OTHELLO [Rising] O, she was foul!

伊阿古 我不过把我自己的意思告诉他；我对他所说的话，已经由他自己证实了。

爱米利娅 可是你有没有对他说她是不贞的？

伊阿古 我对他说过。

爱米利娅 你说谎，一个可憎的、万恶不赦的谎！凭着我的灵魂起誓，一个谎，一个罪恶的谎！她跟凯西奥私通！你说她跟凯西奥私通吗？

伊阿古 跟凯西奥私通，太太。好了好了，收住你的舌头吧。

爱米利娅 我不愿收住我的舌头，我必须说话。夫人在这儿床上给人谋杀了。

众　人 啊，哪会有这样的事！

爱米利娅 都是你造的谣言，引起这场血案。

奥瑟罗 各位不必惊慌，这事情是真的。

葛莱西安诺 真有这样的事，那可奇了！

蒙太诺 啊，骗人的行为！

爱米利娅 诡计！诡计！诡计！我现在想起来了；啊，诡计！那时候我就有些怀疑，我要伤心死了！啊，诡计！诡计！

伊阿古 什么！你疯了吗？快给我回家去！

爱米利娅 各位先生，让我有一个说话的机会。照理我应该服从他，可是现在却不能服从他。也许，伊阿古，我永远不再回家了。

奥瑟罗 啊！啊！啊！

扑卧床上。

爱米利娅 哼，你躺下来哭叫吧，因为你已经杀死一个世间最温柔纯洁的人。

奥瑟罗 啊，她是淫污的！我简直不认识您啦，叔父。那边躺着您的侄

I scarce did know you, uncle: there lies your niece,
Whose breath, indeed, these hands have newly stopp'd:
I know this act shows horrible and grim.

GRATIANO Poor Desdemona! I am glad thy father's dead:
Thy match was mortal to him, and pure grief
Shore his old thread in twain: did he live now,
This sight would make him do a desperate turn,
Yea, curse his better angel from his side,
And fall to reprobation.

OTHELLO 'Tis pitiful; but yet Iago knows
That she with Cassio hath the act of shame
A thousand times committed; Cassio confess'd it:
And she did gratify his amorous works
With that recognizance and pledge of love
Which I first gave her; I saw it in his hand:
It was a handkerchief, an antique token
My father gave my mother.

EMILIA O heaven! O heavenly powers!

IAGO Come, hold your peace.

EMILIA 'Twill out, 'twill out: I peace!
No, I will speak as liberal as the north:
Let heaven and men and devils, let them all,
All, all, cry shame against me, yet I'll speak.

IAGO Be wise, and get you home.

EMILIA I will not.

IAGO offers to stab EMILIA.

GRATIANO Fie! Your sword upon a woman?

EMILIA O thou dull Moor! that handkerchief thou speak'st of
I found by fortune and did give my husband;
For often, with a solemn earnestness,

女，她的呼吸刚才被我这双手扼断；我知道这件行为在世人眼中看起来是惊人而残酷的。

葛莱西安诺 可怜的苔丝狄蒙娜！幸亏你父亲已经死了；你的婚事是他的致死的原因，悲伤摧折了他的衰老的生命。要是他现在还活着，看见这种惨状，一定会干出一些疯狂的事情来的。他会咒天骂地，赶走了身边的守护神，毁灭了自己的灵魂。

奥瑟罗 这诚然是一件伤心的事。可是伊阿古知道她曾经跟凯西奥干过许多回无耻的勾当，凯西奥自己也承认了。她还把我的定情礼物送给凯西奥，作为他殷勤献媚的酬劳。我看见它在他的手里；那是一方手帕，我的父亲给我母亲的一件古老的纪念品。

爱米利娅 天啊！天上的神明啊！

伊阿古 算了，闭住你的嘴！

爱米利娅 事情总会暴露的，事情总会暴露的。闭住我的嘴？不，不，我要像北风一样自由地说话；让天神、世人和魔鬼全都把我嘲骂羞辱，我也要说我的话。

伊阿古 放明白一些，回家去吧。

爱米利娅 我不愿回家。

伊阿古拔剑欲刺爱米利娅。

葛莱西安诺 呸！你向一个妇人动武吗？

爱米利娅 你这愚笨的摩尔人啊！你所说起的那方手帕，是我偶然拾到，把它给了我的丈夫的。虽然那只是一件小小的东西，他却几次三番恳求我替他偷出来。

More than indeed belong'd to such a trifle,
He begg'd of me to steal it.

IAGO Villanous whore!

EMILIA She give it Cassio! no, alas! I found it,
And I did give't my husband.

IAGO Filth, thou liest!

EMILIA By heaven, I do not, I do not, gentlemen.
O murderous coxcomb! what should such a fool
Do with so good a woman?

OTHELLO Are there no stones in heaven
But what serve for the thunder?—Precious villain!

He runs at IAGO,IAGO, from behind, stabs EMILIA, and exit.

GRATIANO The woman falls; sure, he hath kill'd his wife.

EMILIA Ay, ay: O, lay me by my mistress' side.

GRATIANO He's gone, but his wife's kill'd.

MONTANO 'Tis a notorious villain. Take you this weapon,
Which I have here recover'd from the Moor:
Come, guard the door without; let him not pass,
But kill him rather. I'll after that same villain,
For 'tis a damned slave.

Exeunt MONTANO and GRATIANO.

OTHELLO I am not valiant neither,
But ever puny whipster gets my sword:
But why should honour outlive honesty?
Let it go all.

EMILIA What did thy song bode, lady?
Hark, canst thou hear me? I will play the swan.
And die in music.

Singing.

伊 阿 古 长舌的淫妇！

爱米利娅 她送给凯西奥！唉！不，是我拾到了，把它交给我的丈夫的。

伊 阿 古 贱人，你说谎！

爱米利娅 苍天在上，我没有说谎；我没有说谎，各位先生。杀人的傻瓜啊！像你这样一个蠢材，怎么配得上这样好的一位妻子呢？

奥 瑟 罗 天上没有石块，可以像雷霆一样打下来吗？好一个奸贼！

向伊阿古扑奔；伊阿古刺爱米利娅逃下。

葛莱西安诺 这妇人倒下来了。他把他的妻子杀死了。

爱米利娅 是，是，啊！把我放在夫人的身旁吧！

葛莱西安诺 他走了，他的妻子给他杀了。

蒙 太 诺 这是一个罪大恶极的凶徒。你拿着我从这摩尔人手里夺下来的剑。来，在门外看守好了，别让他出去；他要是想逃走，尽管把他杀死。我要去追那恶人，那是一个不可宽恕的家伙。

蒙太诺、葛莱西安诺下。

奥 瑟 罗 我的勇气也离我而去了，每一个孱弱的懦夫都可以夺下我的剑来。可是奸恶既然战胜了正直，哪里还会有荣誉存在呢？让一切都归于幻灭吧！

爱米利娅 你的歌儿是一个谶兆吗，夫人？听，你听没听见我的声音？我要像天鹅一般在歌声中死去。

唱。

Willow, willow, willow,—
Moor, she was chaste; she loved thee, cruel Moor;
So come my soul to bliss, as I speak true;
So speaking as I think, I die, I die.

Dies.

OTHELLO I have another weapon in this chamber;
It is a sword of Spain, the ice-brook's temper:—
O, here it is. Uncle, I must come forth.

GRATIANO *[Within]* If thou attempt it, it will cost thee dear:
Thou hast no weapon, and perforce must suffer.

OTHELLO Look in upon me then and speak with me,
Or, naked as I am, I will assault thee.

Re-enter GRATIANO.

GRATIANO What is the matter?

OTHELLO Behold, I have a weapon;
A better never did itself sustain
Upon a soldier's thigh: I have seen the day,
That, with this little arm and this good sword,
I have made my way through more impediments
Than twenty times your stop: but, O vain boast!
Who can control his fate? 'tis not so now.
Be not afraid, though you do see me weapon'd;
Here is my journey's end, here is my butt,
And very sea-mark of my utmost sail.
Do you go back dismay'd? 'tis a lost fear;
Man but a rush against Othello's breast,
And he retires. Where should Othello go?
Now, how dost thou look now? O ill-starr'd wench!
Pale as thy smock! when we shall meet at compt,

杨柳，杨柳，杨柳……

摩尔人，她是贞洁的；她爱你，狠心的摩尔人。我说的是真话，愿我的灵魂享受天福；我的话是跟我的思想一致的。我死了，我死了。

死。

奥瑟罗 我还有一柄剑在这屋子里，那是一柄用冰泉的水所浸炼的西班牙宝剑。啊，在这儿！叔父，我一定要出来。

葛莱西安诺 （在内）你要是敢试一试，就得付重大的代价；你没有武器，只好屈服。

奥瑟罗 那么进来瞧瞧我吧，我有话对你说；否则我虽然没有武器，也只好不顾一切跟你拼一下了。

葛莱西安诺重上。

葛莱西安诺 什么事？

奥瑟罗 瞧！我有一柄剑，从来没有一个战士佩带过比这更好的剑。凭着这一条小小的胳臂和这一柄利剑，我曾经冲破二十倍于你们这样人数的包围。可是，无聊的夸口啊！谁能主宰他自己的命运呢？现在我已经没有那样的本领了。虽然你看我拿着武器，可是不用害怕，这儿是我的旅途的终点，我的航程的最后的目标。你吓得退走了吗？这是不必要的惊恐；谁只要拿一根灯草向奥瑟罗的胸前刺去，他也会向后退缩的。奥瑟罗应该到什么地方去呢？——啊，让我再看看你的脸吧，薄命的女郎！像你的衬衣一样惨白！我们在天底对簿的时候，你这一副脸色就可以把我的灵魂赶下天堂，让魔鬼把它抓去。你的全身冰冷，我的恋人！正像你的贞洁一样凛若寒霜。啊，该死的、该死的奴才！魔鬼啊，把我从这天仙一样美人的面前鞭逐出去吧！让狂风把我吹卷、硫磺把我熏烤、沸汤的深渊把我沉浸吧！啊，苔丝狄蒙娜！苔丝狄蒙娜！死了！啊！啊！啊！

This look of thine will hurl my soul from heaven,
And fiends will snatch at it. Cold, cold, my girl!
Even like thy chastity. O cursed slave!
Whip me, ye devils,
From the possession of this heavenly sight!
Blow me about in winds! roast me in sulphur!
Wash me in steep-down gulfs of liquid fire!
O Desdemona! Desdemona! dead!
Oh! Oh! Oh!

Enter LODOVICO. MONTANO, CASSIO carried in a chair, and Officers with IAGO,prisoner.

LODOVICO Where is this rash and most unfortunate man?
OTHELLO That's he that was Othello: here I am.
LODOVICO Where is that viper? bring the villain forth.
OTHELLO I look down towards his feet; but that's a fable.
If that thou best a devil, I cannot kill thee.

Wounds IAGO.

LODOVICO Wrench his sword from him.
IAGO I bleed, sir; but not kill'd.
OTHELLO I am not sorry neither: I'ld have thee live;
For, in my sense, 'tis happiness to die.
LODOVICO O thou Othello, thou wert once so good,
Fall'n in the practise of a damned slave,
What shall be said to thee?
OTHELLO Why, any thing:
An honourable murderer, if you will;
For nought I did in hate, but all in honour.
LODOVICO This wretch hath part confess'd his villany:
Did you and he consent in Cassio's death?

罗多维科、蒙太诺，二侍从以卧椅抬凯西奥及吏役等押伊阿古同上。

罗多维科　这鲁莽而不幸的人在哪儿？

奥瑟罗　那就是从前的奥瑟罗；我在这儿。

罗多维科　那条毒蛇呢？把这恶人带上来。

奥瑟罗　据说魔鬼的脚是分趾的，让我看看他的脚是不是这样。要是你真的是一个魔鬼，我也不能杀死你。

刺伤伊阿古。

罗多维科　把他手里的剑夺下来。

伊阿古　我不过流了点儿血，还没有给他杀死。

奥瑟罗　那也好，我要你留着活命。因为在我看来，死倒是一桩幸福。

罗多维科　啊，奥瑟罗！你本来是一个很好的汉子，却会中一个万恶的奸人的诡计，我们该说你什么呢？

奥瑟罗　随便你们怎么说吧。要是你们愿意，不妨说我是一个正直的凶手，因为我所干的事，都是出于荣誉的观念，不是出于猜嫌的私恨。

罗多维科　这恶人已经承认了一部分他的奸谋。杀死凯西奥是你跟他同谋的吗？

OTHELLO Ay.

CASSIO Dear general, I never gave you cause.

OTHELLO I do believe it, and I ask your pardon.
Will you, I pray, demand that demi-devil
Why he hath thus ensnared my soul and body?

IAGO Demand me nothing: what you know, you know:
From this time forth I never will speak word.

LODOVICO What, not to pray?

GRATIANO Torments will ope your lips.

OTHELLO Well, thou dost best.

LODOVICO Sir, you shall understand what hath befall'n,
Which, as I think, you know not. Here is a letter
Found in the pocket of the slain Roderigo;
And here another: the one of them imports
The death of Cassio to be undertook
By Roderigo.

OTHELLO O villain!

CASSIO Most heathenish and most gross!

LODOVICO Now here's another discontented paper,
Found in his pocket too; and this, it seems,
Roderigo meant to have sent this damned villain;
But that belike Iago in the interim
Came in and satisfied him.

OTHELLO O the pernicious caitiff!
How came you, Cassio, by that handkerchief
That was my wife's?

CASSIO I found it in my chamber:
And he himself confess'd but even now
That there he dropp'd it for a special purpose
Which wrought to his desire.

OTHELLO O fool! fool! fool!

奥瑟罗 是的。

凯西奥 主帅，我从来不曾得罪过您。

奥瑟罗 我相信你的话，愿你原谅我吧。你们问一问那个顶着人头的恶魔，为什么他要这样陷害我的灵魂和肉体？

伊阿古 什么也不要问我；你们所知道的，你们已经知道了。从这一刻起，我不再说一句话。

罗多维科 什么！你也不要祈祷吗？

葛莱西安诺 酷刑可以逼你开口。

奥瑟罗 嘿，你这是最好的办法。

罗多维科 将军，一切经过，你将会明白的，我相信你现在还一点也不知道。这是从已死的罗德利哥衣袋里搜到的一封信；这儿还有一封；其中一封信里说到杀死凯西奥的事情由罗德利哥动手执行。

奥瑟罗 啊，奸贼！

凯西奥 野蛮残忍的阴谋！

罗多维科 这儿还有从他的衣袋里找到的一封充满怨言的信，看来好像是罗德利哥预备寄给这个万恶的奸人的，可是信还没有寄出，伊阿古就给了他回答了。

奥瑟罗 啊，恶毒的奸贼！凯西奥，我的妻子的手帕怎么会到你手里的？

凯西奥 我在我的房间里找到它。他刚才已经亲口承认是他有意把它丢在那里的，借此可以达到他自己的图谋。

奥瑟罗 啊，傻瓜！傻瓜！傻瓜！

CASSIO There is besides in Roderigo's letter,
How he upbraids Iago, that he made him
Brave me upon the watch; whereon it came
That I was cast: and even but now he spake,
After long seeming dead, Iago hurt him,
Iago set him on.

LODOVICO You must forsake this room, and go with us:
Your power and your command is taken off,
And Cassio rules in Cyprus. For this slave,
If there be any cunning cruelty
That can torment him much and hold him long,
It shall be his. You shall close prisoner rest,
Till that the nature of your fault be known
To the Venetian state. Come, bring him away.

OTHELLO Soft you; a word or two before you go.
I have done the state some service, and they know't.
No more of that. I pray you, in your letters,
When you shall these unlucky deeds relate,
Speak of me as I am; nothing extenuate,
Nor set down aught in malice: then must you speak
Of one that loved not wisely but too well;
Of one not easily jealous, but being wrought
Perplex'd in the extreme; of one whose hand,
Like the base Indian, threw a pearl away
Richer than all his tribe; of one whose subdued eyes,
Albeit unused to the melting mood,
Drop tears as fast as the Arabian trees
Their medicinal gum. Set you down this;
And say besides, that in Aleppo once,
Where a malignant and a turban'd Turk
Beat a Venetian and traduced the state,

凯 西 奥　在罗德利哥的信里，他又埋怨伊阿古不该撺掇他在我值夜的时候向我寻事；我就是为了那一回事情而去职的。就在刚才，他从长时间的昏迷中醒了过来，还说起他一切都受伊阿古的指使，结果却是伊阿古伤了他的生命。

罗多维科　你必须离开这所屋子，跟我们去；你的军队和兵权必须全部交卸，让凯西奥主持塞浦路斯的军政重务。对于这一个家伙，我们将要用一切巧妙的酷刑加在他的身上，使他遍受种种的痛苦，而不至于立刻死去。我们还要把你严密监禁，等候威尼斯政府判决你的罪状。来，把他带下去。

奥 瑟 罗　且慢，在你们未走以前，再听我说一两句话。我对于国家曾经立过相当的功劳，这是执政诸公所知道的。那些话现在也不用说了。当你们把这种不幸的事实报告他们的时候，请你们在公文上老老实实照我本来的样子叙述，不要徇情回护，也不要恶意构陷；你们应当说我是一个在恋爱上不智而过于深情的人；一个不容易发生嫉妒的人，可是一旦被人煽动以后，就会糊涂到极点；一个像印度人一样糊涂的人，会把一颗比他整个部落所有的财产更贵重的珍珠随手抛弃；一个不惯于流妇人之泪的人，可是当他被感情征服的时候，也会像涌流着胶液的阿拉伯胶树一般两眼泛滥。请你们把这些话记下，再补充一句说：在阿勒坡地方，曾经有一个裹着头巾的敌意的土耳其人殴打一个威尼斯人，诽谤我们的国家，那时候我就一把抓住这受割礼的狗子的咽喉，就这样把他杀了。

I took by the throat the circumcised dog,
And smote him, thus.

Stabs himself.

LODOVICO O bloody period!

GRATIANO All that's spoke is marr'd.

OTHELLO I kiss'd thee ere I kill'd thee: no way but this;
Killing myself, to die upon a kiss.

Falling upon Desdemona, and dies.

CASSIO This did I fear, but thought he had no weapon;
For he was great of heart.

LODOVICO *[To IAGO]* O Spartan dog,
More fell than anguish, hunger, or the sea!
Look on the tragic loading of this bed;
This is thy work: the object poisons sight;
Let it be hid. Gratiano, keep the house,
And seize upon the fortunes of the Moor,
For they succeed on you. To you, lord governor,
Remains the censure of this hellish villain;
The time, the place, the torture: O, enforce it!
Myself will straight aboard: and to the state
This heavy act with heavy heart relate.

Exeunt.

以剑自刎。

罗多维科 啊，残酷的结局！

葛莱西安诺 一切说过的话，现在又要颠倒过来了。

奥 瑟 罗 我在杀死你以前，曾经用一吻和你诀别；现在我自己的生命也在一吻里终结。

倒扑在苔丝狄蒙娜身上，死。

凯 西 奥 我早就担心会有这样的事发生，可是我还以为他没有武器；他的心地是光明正大的。

罗多维科 （向伊阿古）你这比痛苦、饥饿和大海更凶暴的猛犬啊！瞧瞧这床上一双浴血的尸身吧，这是你干的好事。这样伤心惨目的景象，赶快把它遮盖起来吧。葛莱西安诺，请您接收这一座屋子，这摩尔人的全部家产，都应该归您继承。总督大人，怎样处置这一个恶魔般的奸徒，什么时候，什么地点，用怎样的刑法，都要请您全权办理，千万不要宽纵他！我现在就要上船回去禀明政府，用一颗悲哀的心报告这一段悲哀的事故。

同下。